Get Rich, Stay Rich

. . . and become financially free

Martin Hawes and Joan Baker

Martin and Joan welcome comments on this and
their other books. They can be contacted at:
<mhawes@wealthcoaches.net>
<jbaker@wealthcoaches.net>

First published in 2003

This South Asian Edition Published in 2004

Allen & Unwin
83 Alexander Street
Crows Nest NSW 2065
Australia
Phone: (61 2) 8425 0100
Fax: (61 2) 9906 2218
Email: info@allenandunwin.com
Web: www.allenandunwin.com

National Library of Australia
Cataloguing-in-Publication entry:

Hawes, Martin, 1952– .
Get rich, stay rich . . . and become financially free.

ISBN 1 74114 105 2.

1. Finance, Personal. 2. Saving and investment. I. Baker
Joan, 1956– . II. Title.

332.02401

This edition is for sale in India, Bangladesh, Pakistan, Sri Lanka & Nepal only. Not for export elsewhere.

Set in 12/14 pt A Garamond by Bookhouse, Sydney
Printed and bound in India by
Replika Press Pvt. Ltd., Kundli 131 028

Contents

Introduction

Wealth creation is an act of love. Money and riches are not important in themselves. The first thing you need to understand about *Get Rich, Stay Rich* is that money is only important in that it can let you do the things you love, and look after the people you love. If you do not have these outcomes as part of your dream, there is no point in creating wealth and becoming rich. To set out to make a lot of money for its own sake, without a bigger goal, is to doom yourself to a life of disappointment.

Riches only have meaning insofar as they can allow you and the people around you a bigger and better life. In this respect, creating financial freedom is an act of love—a show of love of yourself (you're worth it), a show of love of those things that you like to do, and a show of love of those around you.

You *can* be wealthy and financially free—the things that are necessary for you to create wealth are either doable or learnable, and there is nothing that cannot be overcome stopping you from having the life that you want. With a powerful dream and the willingness to act, you can join that group of people who live life on their own terms, in the way they want to live.

There are no silver bullets, however—this book is not a get-rich-quick scheme. Most get-rich-quick schemes are scams, designed to fleece the gullible, those who think that there is a shortcut to riches. If we knew of a quick and honest way to riches that didn't involve much effort, we would write a book on it . . . promise! But we don't. And we don't because there is no such thing. Wealth creation takes time. It also takes hard work and homework.

Certainly you have to have a dream of wealth. But you cannot simply daydream your way to riches—you have to act, taking time to plan, assess and analyse both the market and yourself, and be prepared to fill in the gaps in terms of the knowledge and skills that you may not have.

The soft skills of wealth creation (self-belief, motivation, attitude) are important, and are a key part of this book. But in themselves they are not enough. You also need financial acumen, the hard skills of money that means knowing your way around the ideas and jargon of finance, investment and business. You have to raise your financial quotient. The right attitude and motivation, essential though they are, are not enough by themselves.

Getting rich, staying rich and being free is good—there is nothing wrong with wealth. In spite of what some might say, there is no virtue in being poor. Wealth lets you do things; it gives you choices. Wealth allowes you to devote your time to worthwhile causes or to rescue family members when they need it. Many of the things that we value as individuals, communities and societies depend on wealth and the people who create it. As individuals and communities, we must have surpluses, more than what we need to just survive, in order to realise our own potential, to be able to put our time and effort into philanthropical worthwhile ventures, and to create opportunities for others. With wealth you can make a greater contribution—to yourself, your family and your community.

Financial freedom is a great game—learn to play this game to win. Forget the get-rich-quick schemes, and stop trying to day-dream your way to wealth. There are well-worn paths to abundance that are achievable, admirable and lots of fun. Read on—you can have the life that you want.

Joan Baker
Martin Hawes

Part I

Getting the life you want

Chapter 1 | Financial freedom is not for everyone

This book is different. It is not like any of the others we have written.

In the past, all of our work has been geared towards people with fairly conventional goals—people who want to develop their careers, be more successful, manage their money a little better, save money on their mortgages and learn to invest. Most people do not want much more than this—a nice comfortable life without big dreams and big efforts to attain those dreams is just fine.

Most of our work over the years has been to show these people how to repay debt quickly, and then build a store of wealth through a diversified portfolio containing good solid investments. We believe passionately in the general process of paying off debt and then investing safely for most people. The idea of getting rid of the mortgage and then spreading savings around a range of solid and diversified investments works well. It may not be spectacular, it may not make you rich, but not everyone sets out with riches and financial freedom in mind. Most people want to feel safe and secure, perhaps do a bit better than average, but not much more than that.

That approach is right for most people—but this book is different. This book is not for most people. A good solid diversified portfolio works well, but it will not make you rich or financially free. It has a part to play in financial freedom (a very important part) but it will not take you to financial freedom.

Paying off the mortgage before investing, then investing in super funds and the like will increase your wealth by around 5 per cent a year. If you follow the usual pattern of repaying debt, then making steady investments, you will not go far wrong.

If you combine this with adopting many of the ideas that we have talked about over the last decade or so on growing wealth, careers and business, you will do a bit better than 'all right' and have a nice comfortable lifestyle. We have presented seminars and written many books and articles, both together and individually on these subjects. We have always been delighted with helping people learn to manage their money and their lives better and to become better off in the process.

But there are people who want more than just a nice comfortable lifestyle—those whose dream of a bigger life includes more than being rich and achieveing financial freedom. Becoming wealthy involves more than simply repaying debt and finding a good super fund. This book is for those who dream of being financially free.

To achieve the riches and financial freedom we are talking about is not easy, and does require sacrifice. In our experience, only a few will make the commitment that is necessary. You will not be stopped from achieving a high goal by the lack of any particular ability—but you do have to *want* it. And you have to want it a lot! More than anything, we have found that it is the desire and the commitment that makes the difference—and the first thing you need to do is decide what your dreams are, what sort of life you want, and whether you are prepared to put in the effort to achieve it.

The ideas in this book come from nearly 20 years of giving business and financial advice. Over the past couple of years we have taken on a small number of clients who have wanted to become financially free, and who wanted to be coached to achieve their dreams and goals. The good things that have happened, and some of the bad, have taught us much about how to achieve financial freedom.

The biggest principle behind achieving financial freedom is that you must first *really* want it. People who succeed in reaching this goal do not do so because they have greater financial skills or some sort of inside knowledge (although these things are necessary)—the real difference is that they have powerful dreams and great motivation and drive. If your desire is strong enough, nothing will stop you—there are no natural impediments that cannot be overcome, nothing that cannot be learned. If you do not *really* want to be rich, then you will find it hard to become so, no matter how astounding your abilities. The so-called 'soft' skills of vision, motivation, determination, attitude and desire are very important, and the hardest to learn and adopt.

Anyone can become financially free—but you have to know what it is you want and you have to want it enough. If you do not, you will have neither the ability to do some of the hard stuff that is necessary, nor the 'stickability' to keep on going. You cannot go into this half-heartedly. You must decide either, to go all out for financial freedom, giving it all your commitment and energy, or to stick with repaying the mortgage, a good solid diversified portfolio and a comfortable and easy lifestyle.

The interesting thing about money is that there is no single approach that is right for everyone—we all have different dreams in life (and therefore financial goals), and different strategies need to be employed to meet different goals. If your goal is to move up and above the crowd to financial freedom, if you are different, read on.

Chapter 2 | Having it all!

The conference was into its second day before we were due to make our presentation. The theme was 'Wealth Creation' and the 200 attendees had already heard from several speakers giving their ideas on how to become wealthy. There were a couple of people who had talked about property investment, doing up properties and property development, and someone else had given a very upbeat talk on the money that he had made trading shares and options. Someone else had outlined his activity of buying, building up and then selling businesses, with examples of big profits in very short periods of time.

The attendees could have been forgiven if they thought that they could leave the conference and be rich within a few weeks. Certainly, we admired all these people who had given up a lot to be there—travelled to the Gold Coast and paid big fees to attend. We knew that some of their ideas would work out, but also knew that it would not be as easy as it sounded. Our experience has taught us that it was perfectly possible to get rich—but harder to stay rich, and harder still to be free.

Our presentation was different—we talked about 'Getting Rich and Staying Rich—Creating Freedom for the Life You Want'. We too were very focused on the ways that people could create wealth and grow their net worth. After all, this is why people were at the conference—they wanted to know the secrets and skills of becoming rich.

And there is lots to know, ranging from how to choose an activity that will make you rich, to learning how to drive that wealth-creating activity for super-profits. We outlined the insights we had gleaned from coaching and consulting with successful wealth creators. The successful have many similarities. Those who succeed in creating wealth through business, property or the markets know a lot of stuff that the unsuccessful do not. The good news is that this stuff is learnable—and we spent time outlining the key things that you need to know.

Where we differed with many of the other presentations was in our emphasis on becoming **free**. Believe it or not, it isn't all that difficult to create wealth. But the point of having wealth is that it allows you to have the life you want, to live out your dreams. Ensuring that you keep the wealth that you create—that your wealth is sustainable—is the key to success. There is no point in becoming 'rich' if you can never stop! Many people have found ways to create a lot of income—but it often takes them 70 hours a week, they can never leave the business/farm/clients, and the income stops when they do! Many wealth-creating activities are very exposed so that people live in constant fear of the next drought/recession/client defection. It doesn't sound like great fun—and it isn't. People want to be rich but they also want to be free to enjoy their lives, keep their health, and use their wealth.

After our session we were approached by two people who asked if they could buy us a drink and have a chat. They were a married couple living in Melbourne, aged about 30. Kevin was an architectural draftsman and Colleen was a landscape designer. They wanted to become rich. They were committed to being wealthy by the age of 45 and wanted to spend the rest of their lives painting, travelling, and studying art. Their dreams would require quite a lot of money—they wanted to pursue their future artistic lives in some comfort. They related very strongly to the notion of being 'free'—while they already had high incomes they were 'trapped' by long hours, demanding assignments, and the continual worry of a downturn in demand for their services. They understood that high incomes are not enough to be free—you have to have enough income so that you don't have to go to the coalface every day, forever. They wanted to know how they could make enough money to give them sufficient income to be free for the rest of their lives. Good employment gives cash flow, but you can never get away from it and never create a capital asset—you can't sell a career! Kevin and Colleen could develop their careers, make very high incomes on the way, and live a privileged lifestyle, but they did not want to have to work at their careers for the rest of their days. What to do?

Well, Kevin and Colleen had a great advantage in that they were clear about what they wanted in their lives, they were serious about making it happen and they were prepared to do whatever it takes. We asked lots of questions to find out more about them, what other knowledge and experiences they had, what else they might be able to do.

We found a piece of paper and started sketching out their plan as we went. We looked first at their wealth creation, and put that at the top of the page:

What would Kevin and Colleen use to create wealth? At present they only had good incomes from good jobs—plenty to live on but not really wealth-creating by itself. We discussed several options:

1. Setting up some kind of business, for example, around one of their careers, or in something related. They were unenthusiastic about this idea, claiming that while they enjoyed their work and were clearly good at what they did, they had no belief in themselves running consultancy businesses. They liked doing the work but wanted their respective employers to continue to find the clients, manage the business and pay them a salary. In any event, a business based on their professions would be unlikely to become very valuable.

2. Using their high incomes to trade in shares. Colleen was interested (she had taken a finance paper as part of her training) but Kevin was very nervous, as his parents had lost almost everything in 1987 after mortgaging their home to invest in the booming share market of the time. (Not an unusual story.)
3. Becoming active property investors. Kevin and Colleen had already expressed an interest in do-ups and they should certainly have at least some of the skills necessary to assess and improve properties. Their eyes lit up. We discussed the fact that this would need to be treated in a very business-like way—there is more to making money through property than doing up lovely old villas! They did not know much about the business side of trading in property but they were keen to learn. That was enough—after all, it isn't rocket science!

We had found the right activity—property investment. Property would be their 'Wealth-creating Asset'. This was the thing that they were going to drive hard and aggressively, the thing that would give high enough returns to create real wealth quickly. Kevin and Colleen committed to learning what they needed to know to become aggressive traders in property—they would have to learn to buy well, to manage tenants, to increase the property value, to know the market . . .

Where was their income to come from? Their well-paying jobs—they were already earning $70 000 after tax between them. We put 'Income' at the bottom of the page.

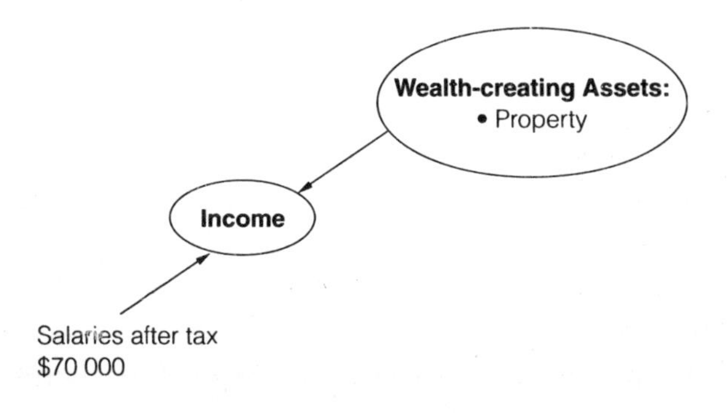

'Well, some of that will go into consumption,' we said. 'You have to buy the groceries and live. What does it cost you for rent, cars and weekly living?' They weren't certain, so we made an estimate of $40 000 and suggested that they do some work to more precisely assess their costs and develop a consumption plan for the future.

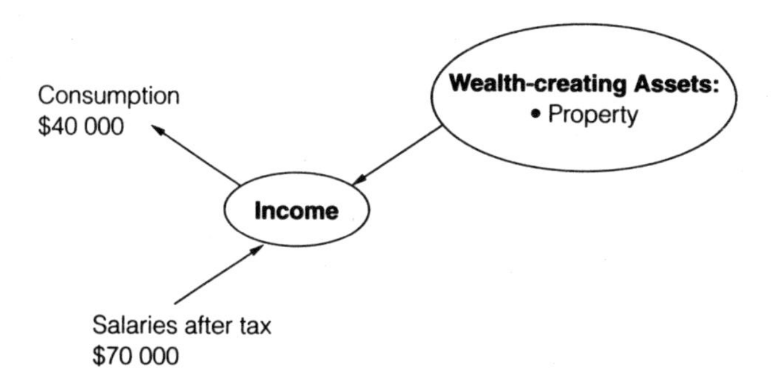

'Will you put all of your spare income into wealth creating activities?' we asked.

'Yes, all of it,' they answered. 'We want to grow the business and our property as quickly as possible.'

'Okay,' we said. 'Let's leave that for the moment. What about your security?'

Security? This stopped them—they hadn't thought of that. What did they want to protect their assets for? After all, they were going to have plenty of money. With their property activities they didn't need to think of security.

'But that is critical,' we said. 'You need assets tucked away, quarantined from your more risky activities. It's your store of wealth, your fallback position if something goes wrong. This is what allows you to ride out the difficult times and be resilient in your business activities. And, when you have created considerable wealth it will be these assets that will give you the passive income that you want for your lifestyle.'

We wrote 'Security Assets' as the third point of the triangle.

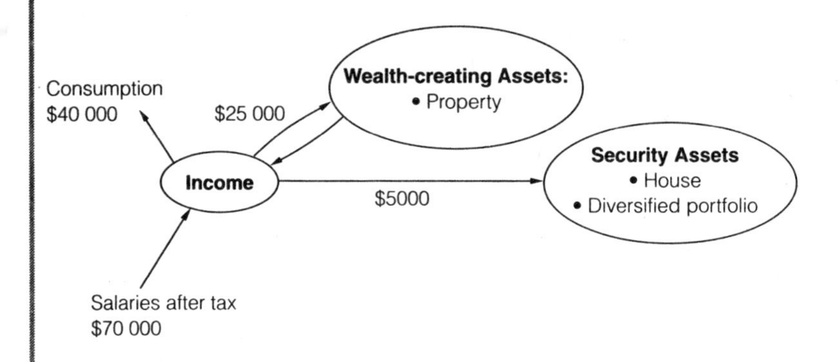

This couple needed what all entrepreneurs need, a plan that would allow them to become wealthy. They had that—they were going to invest in property. But just as important, they needed a plan that would give them the passive income that would allow them to stay rich and be free to pursue their dreams. Kevin and Colleen would need to do some work to fill in the numbers—create a budget for their property/business and consumption—but now they had a model or template that they could work with. But first they had another question:

'What would we have as Security Assets?' they asked.

First of all would be the house. They had bought a modest home the year before which was mortgaged for two-thirds of its value. They were already paying off the mortgage—we thought they should continue to do that . . . What then? We discussed the benefits of starting to build a diversified portfolio. While this was seemingly the antithesis of wealth creation, we talked about the importance of diversifying investment, and using fund managers to get exposure to offshore markets and areas of commercial activity other than property (they would already be heavily weighted in property). We showed how to get a spread of investments tailored to their own situation and circumstances, and how that strategy should give an annual after-tax return of perhaps 5 per cent over a long period. The diversified portfolio, while unexciting, is a key part of the plan for financial freedom. While it seldom makes people rich, it is the most bullet-proof, indestructible store of wealth ever devised.

What Kevin and Colleen were trying to do—create wealth through entrepreneurship—was a worthy goal, but we knew from experience that a bit of success early on is likely to lead to feelings of invulnerability—which in turn could lead them to plough everything they had made back into their property investments. When people do this, in effect they are playing 'double or quits'; that is, everything they owned is in one asset and everything they make goes back into that asset. If Kevin and Colleen fell into that trap, keeping all their wealth in highly geared property, they would only be as good as their last deal—one mistake and they would be gone.

This is where the diversified portfolio shows its value as part of the wealth-creation strategy. Building up Security Assets in the form of good safe diversified investments does not produce spectacular returns, but Kevin and Colleen's funds would be secure, and they would be able to draw passive income from them for the rest of their lives, reliably, and without the need to drive their assets hard on a continual basis.

We recommended that they siphon off 10 per cent of their income (salaries plus rental income) into paying off the mortgage and, when that is gone, into a diversified portfolio each year. This would both insulate some of their wealth and begin to build up a store of wealth that would eventually provide income in mid-life and beyond. As they increased their net worth and neared the end of their wealth-creation phase we recommended they divert a greater proportion of their income into their Security Assets.

•

Most people who set out to become rich know how they expect to do it, and plan for success. But you need to plan for the challenges as well. There is nothing surer than that you will meet with mishap from time to time. If you keep doing anything for long enough, eventually you will face some real challenges.

The secret of survival is to ensure that those challenges (the misfortunes that are visited on us all) will not be fatal, that they will not destroy everything you have built up. If you keep ploughing everything you make back into your business or your property investments, you have no fallback position. Those who make it to financial freedom come with the attitude that to be able to thrive, they must first be able to survive, and thus arrange their affairs in such a way that their mistakes and challenges (inevitable) will not be fatal. This is a different way of thinking—one that was displayed by few at the conference, where 'quick fix' and 'get rich quick' thinking prevailed.

You can if you wish put everything back into your Wealth-creating Assets (your business or property or shares) but remember when you do so that you are effectively playing 'double or quits'. You are putting everything that you have into one area—one mistake and you are out of the game. Staying in the game is critical. Also remember that from time to time you will need money in a hurry, and this can be a problem if everything you have is tied up in your wealth-creating activity. And if the worst happens in your wealth-creating venture, you have to be able to get back in the game. Your Security Assets can provide the stake that will allow you to start over again. It's important to plan for the long haul. You won't get rich and free overnight—it may take ten to 20 years. You have to plan well and manage well to play for that length of time.

To be financially free you have to build up Security Assets, enough to give you the passive income that will allow you to afford the lifestyle you want. To be financially free is to be free of worry about money or work, to carry little risk. It is a wonderful dream and goal, worth all of the struggle it takes to achieve. Those people who 'have it all' will have thought through their plan and followed it to the end.

Chapter 3 | What is financial freedom?

Financial freedom is not simply being rich. There are many rich people who are not financially free, although you certainly need to be wealthy to have financial freedom. However, having a lot of assets or wealth is not enough by itself. To have financial freedom, that wealth must be invested in areas that will give you passive income. You cannot be free if you still have to work for your money and/or your money is still at risk.

Financial freedom is having enough to afford the lifestyle that you want without having to work or actively manage investments. It is having investments that will produce enough passive income to give you the life that you choose. Being *rich* is having a lot of capital; being *financially free* is having a lot of capital in things that will give you income safely and continuously. The goal is not simply being 'rich', but using your riches to give you enough passive income to achieve your dreams, and give it to you reliably. Those who are rich and financially free know that they will stay rich. Without sufficient passive income from secure investments you will never be free to live your dreams or pursue your priorities. Without your assets being securely invested, you run the risk of losing wealth (even losing the lot). Therefore, to have financial freedom you must get yourself into a position where you have enough capital in stable investments to give you the passive income that you need. This is obviously quite different from being rich, where your considerable wealth is tied up in a business, highly geared property or a farm.

Passive income is income that you receive while you are having lunch, on the golf course, rock climbing, at home or asleep. It comes from assets that you need do nothing with to produce income. These assets are investments that have no (or at least very little) borrowings so that you are secure in your position. Financial freedom is having enough in good solid investments (well diversified) to be able to live the rest of your life how you want.

The diversified portfolio, then, is quite obviously still important—it is not the way that you will *become* wealthy, but it is the *basis* of being financially free. This is the thing that confuses so many people, who fail to distinguish between what will make them rich (Wealth-creating Assets) and what will give them secure passive income (Security Assets). The two are usually quite different.

People who are rich but who are not financially free include:

- People who own a business, even a big and very successful business, but who are still tied to it and cannot leave it for any period of time.
- People who own investment property with large amounts of borrowing that still needs very active management.
- Farmers, who often have a very high net worth, but who cannot leave the management of the farm for more than a few days and are still subject to all the risks inherent in farming (commodity prices, exchange rates, weather and so on).

If these people do a Net Worth statement they will be worth millions of dollars—but their wealth is not in the right things to give them financial freedom. Unless they cash themselves up (and put the proceeds from the sale into good passive investments) they are at risk, by no means secure, and therefore they are not free. You could say that they have the means or the wealth for financial freedom, but have not chosen to become free.

Other people who give the appearance of being wealthy in fact are a long way from financial freedom. They have good careers that yield them high incomes. They have very nice cars (company provided, of course) and a good house in a good area (often with a big mortgage). This is not financial freedom either—as soon as they stop work, the income stops too. Most have no (or little) assets and investments to provide passive income unless they have diverted a good part of their salaries to investment (and few seem to do that to any great extent).

Being rich is a capital game. It is having a lot of capital, not just a lot of income. To have financial freedom, the income that you have must be achieved passively, not by actively working for it. You only get significant passive income if you have a lot of capital. To be free, your income has to come from *capital* invested, not your *time* invested.

Many people become rich, but too many do not stay rich. Putting all of your wealth back into your business (or into property investments or developments) will expose you to a downturn. Whatever it is that makes you rich is likely to be risky. Achieving financial freedom is about developing wealth from your wealth-creating activity and progressively shifting that wealth into assets that are much more secure and far less exposed to the many vicissitudes that face the activities that create the wealth.

Financial freedom comes down to time and money—you have freedom when your time is your own, and so is your money. You do not have to spend time generating an income, and your money is secure.

You therefore need to think about and plan for two things: *how to get rich,* and *how to stay rich.*

Chapter 4 | Capitalism is the name of the game

Being rich is not about having a lot of income, it is about having a lot of capital. The ultimate aim of financial freedom comes through having a lot of income, but this has to be passive income—that is, income that you get without having to work. Passive income can only come from capital, thus you have to grow your capital (your wealth) to get that passive income.

This sounds simple enough; there is not a lot that is complicated about it. However, many people confuse a high income with being rich. High income earners can give every appearance of being rich (they have all the toys and trappings of the rich), but most often they are not. Being rich is about having capital, capital that can be converted into assets that will give you passive income. Having lots of capital is the final objective—capitalism is the name of the game. You have to be an owner—an owner of the right things.

What you do with your income during the time you are trying to get rich is important. A lot of people manage to get high incomes from their businesses or investment activities but some of them, because of how they use this income, do not get rich.

Income has four important uses:

- **Consumption** You have to live.
- **Reinvestment** If you retain income (that is, you do not spend it) it is added to your capital and will grow. When income is added to a Wealth-creating Asset, interest will compound at a higher rate and your capital will grow very quickly.
- **It pays for borrowings** Nearly everyone who becomes rich gears up the capital they have by borrowing. Borrowing

reduces the amount of your disposable income (because you have to pay interest) but increases the growth of your capital (because by borrowing you have increased your Wealth-creating Assets).

- **Setting capital value** The income you get from your capital sets the values of your assets. Regardless of whether the asset is a business, shares or property, its value is set by the amount of income that comes from it. Thus, increasing the amount of income from your Wealth-creating Assets (business, property investments, etc.) increases their value.

To become rich to grow your capital quickly, you need to own Wealth-creating Assets. These are things that will give a *total* return (capital growth plus income) of at least 15% p.a. on your money; anything less and your wealth will not grow quickly enough to make you rich. Only three things give that sort of return:

- a business (this includes farms);
- property; and
- growth shares.

To get rich you have to own something from one of these three categories. This is what you will have your capital in, what you will get your income from and what will make you wealthy. If you can average 15% p.a. from your business or other activities, you will become rich (but you cannot continue to own these things if you want financial freedom). To get a 15 per cent return from your Wealth-creating Assets, you will have to manage what you own actively and take risks. As we discussed in the previous chapter, active management (that is, work) and being in a high-risk situation is not our idea of financial freedom. We cannot stress enough that to become financially free you first need to become rich (have a lot of capital) through some risky enterprise, then over time move that capital into something that will give passive income with low risk.

The first thing to think about is how to get rich.

Chapter 5 | The 'virtuous circle' of wealth

Although having a lot of income is not in itself being rich, income is critical to becoming rich. To become rich you must generate a lot of income from your Wealth-creating Assets, and use this income wisely and well.

Financially astute people who achieve an increase in their income celebrate. When you have a good year with your business and the annual profit increases, when you manage to increase the rents on your properties, when the companies that you have invested in increase their earnings and dividends, you are happy, and you celebrate. That your income has increased is very good news.

However, the increased income is not good news in itself. Sure, the extra money is useful, and you could take it out and spend it. But if you are serious about getting rich you would not do that. The increased income itself is not so terribly important—rather, it is what that extra income can do for you that is important.

It is the attitude towards increased income that distinguishes the successful from the unsuccessful. Those who are never likely to become free tend to look at the extra income and think about what they can spend it on—another overseas holiday, a boat, increase the mortgage on the house to build a swimming pool. If you are determined to be rich and successful you will view the extra income quite differently: instead of thinking about what you can do with this extra income, you will think about what the extra income can do for you. Instead of thinking about the 'fun' that you might have with the additional money, you will be thinking about its effect on your financial position and the extra opportunities it has brought you.

This difference in attitude towards income is one element of the divide between those who will become rich and free, and those who will not. Those who will not achieve financial freedom think only of consumption.

To achieve financial freedom you need to think of your income in two particular ways:

Extra income means your assets will have a higher value

All Wealth-creating Assets are valued by the income they generate—the family business is valued by the profits it makes; property investments by the rent they bring in; and shares by their earnings (in much the same way as the family business). Someone who owns a small commercial property might be able to increase the rent by $5000 a year, and celebrate not because of the extra income and its spending power but because the value of the property is now greater (perhaps by as much as $50 000). The extra income from rent (or business profits) increases the value of the asset because a prospective purchaser would agree to pay more for it to get the higher income. The extra income means that you have become richer (you have more capital worth). This additional capital growth is often worth several times the additional income that was generated.

Extra income can be used to borrow against

Not only will you have higher capital values to use as security, but you will also have more income to fund borrowings. The ability to borrow more means that you can dramatically increase the total amount invested in your Wealth-creating Assets. This in turn will generate even more income, spinning the 'virtuous circle' of wealth even faster. This is, of course, the compounding effect—it is no less potent for Wealth-creating Assets such as, businesses, farms, property and share portfolios than it is for other investments. (In fact it is more potent because the returns are even higher.)

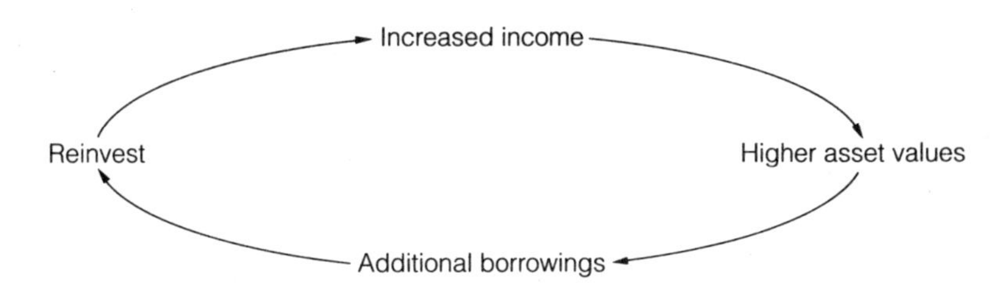

The critical factor here is your attitude to your income, and in particular to the increases in income that you achieve. If you simply spend it, consume it in one way or the other, it is gone—it is out of the system. If you are determined to get rich you will keep it in the system, ploughing it back to keep the 'virtuous circle' of wealth turning for your future benefit. You use the extra capital in your businesses to buy new plant and equipment, increase stock levels, add a new product range or division, or you purchase more investment property or shares. You reinvest, continuing to strive to grow your wealth at 15 per cent or greater, compounding your returns into riches.

Your attitude to your income, your understanding of how your income can become capital which in turn gets more income, is critical. People become rich because they handle their income well—they have a plan for their income and they work the plan. They work very hard to get more income out of their businesses and properties, not for its own sake but for how it grows their capital. The rich use the 'virtuous circle' to grow their wealth with each turn.

Chapter 6 | The 'vicious spiral' of bankruptcy

This is the 'but wait' chapter—the one that sounds a note of caution. It is a chapter warning you that the 'virtuous circle' of wealth can sometimes go too fast, spin out of control into the 'vicious spiral' of bankruptcy. If you play double or quits for long enough, at some point you will come up quits.

There are risks involved in chasing high returns. There are risks involved in being in business (just look at the statistics on how many fail), risks in highly geared property, risks from shares and any other high-return endeavour that you might try. To become rich you have to look for high returns—but remember that high returns come with high risk. At any point the Circle of Wealth can be broken, and send you into a downward 'vicious spiral' towards insolvency.

It is not just that Wealth-creating Assets are risky. They are, of course, but these risks are exacerbated and magnified by the two key components of the Circle of Wealth, borrowings and reinvestment.

Borrowings

Nobody gets rich without borrowing to buy income-earning assets. Gearing or leverage is a necessary part of getting rich as it greatly increases the return you will get on your own capital. You will have to get used to the idea that you will have to borrow to become wealthy—but also realise that while borrowing greatly increases the returns on your capital, if things go the wrong way it also greatly increases your losses. Gearing or leverage speed up your progress to wealth—but of course, the faster you go, the bigger the mess if things go wrong.

Reinvestment

You will be tempted to reinvest all the surplus back into your Wealth-creating Assets—to expand the business, to buy more property or shares. But in doing so you are ploughing everything back into just one area—certainly, a high-performing area but one that you know to be risky (where the risks may already be accentuated by high borrowings). Reinvesting all the extra income in the asset leaves you with the opposite of a diversified portfolio. You are playing double or quits, and you are playing for the family's fortunes.

•

These two things, borrowings and reinvestment, the very things that drive the Circle of Wealth, are at the same time the circle's Achilles heel. The two things that will help you *get rich* are the things that may not let you *stay rich.*

The Circle of Wealth will give you success for a time. When the circle turns well and your reinvested profits are further leveraged with debt, your income and wealth increase hand in hand. But such success is your greatest enemy: it leads to over-confidence and feelings of invulnerability. Many entrepreneurs cannot imagine that they will ever have a failure and keep reinvesting everything they make, gearing up further for even more wealth.

When the Circle of Wealth stops these people are shocked. They have planned only for success with no thought of failure. They have no fallback position, nothing outside their Wealth-creating Assets—which are now caught in a downward 'vicious spiral'. If there is nothing in Security Assets, this is a spiral that is very hard to stop.

Over-confidence is the greatest problem. When things are going well, it seems impossible to imagine them turning bad, there seems to be no need to think about what might happen if the Circle of Wealth stops turning.

Things can go wrong in business and investment for all sorts of reasons: sometimes it is the owner's fault, sometimes it is not. Often the entrepreneur has tried to go too far too fast, gearing up to grow the business or buy more shares or property only to be caught in an economic or industry downturn coupled with a hike in interest rates. A Circle of Wealth, with all profits being reinvested and with ever-higher levels of borrowing, can quickly turn into a downward spiral: income starts to fall, asset values fall with it, cash is difficult to find and the lower asset values means that the gearing rate (the proportion of borrowings to assets) climbs. The owner becomes a forced or distressed seller, which means that asset values are crystallised at a level even lower than expected. Before long, the spiral has the owner out of the game, perhaps pushed by the bank, maybe jumping before the bank has to start pushing.

What can you do about this 'vicious spiral'? Well, once it starts happening, not much. Falling income and asset values are hard to turn around. In most markets, things will eventually come right, but that will take time. If you can survive the bad time, you may thrive in the next economic upswing. However, most entrepreneurs who get caught in the spiral have nothing to get them through to the next upswing except the very businesses and investments that are the cause of their problems.

Once the 'vicious spiral' starts there is not much you can do. The time to manage a downturn is before it starts—when times are good rather than when they have already turned bad. You know that in your drive for financial freedom that there will be tough times—you are bound to have to survive at least one and perhaps several. There will be times when business and investment conditions are difficult, when income falls and interest payments are hard to find. You know that this will happen—it is inevitable. You have to stop playing double or quits, stop entrusting everything you have to the performance of one asset. *You need a plan to lower the stakes.*

Chapter 7 | Planning to survive so that you can thrive

You need to use the 'virtuous circle' of wealth but at the same time guard against the 'vicious spiral' of bankruptcy. We have developed a plan (or model) that can be used by anyone to develop successful financial strategies. This model helps you go on the offensive to create wealth while still having some 'defence plays'.

Our model to get rich and stay rich is a triangular template that lets you plan for financial freedom; that allows you to thrive in the good times and survive the bad times. It is a model for optimism (to get rich) and a model for realism (to stay rich) as well. It allows you to plan and structure your affairs to achieve financial freedom without being stopped halfway through by financial adversity. It is a plan that means that you will be able to survive the bad times so that you are still there to thrive in the good times. In order to win it is not enough to be able to play on the offence; you have to play a good defence game as well.

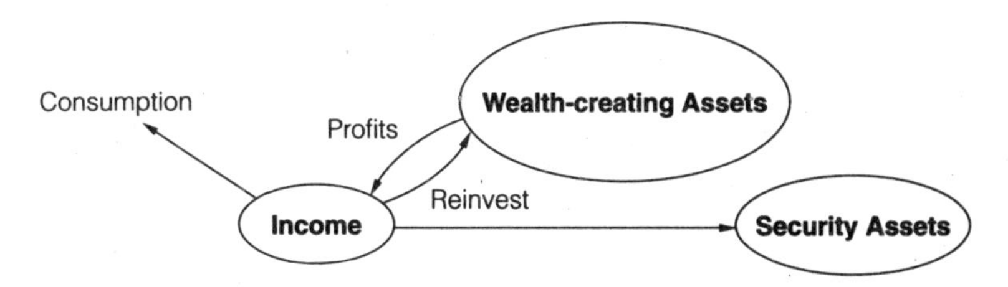

There is much more on how this model works in Part II: Dreams, Goals and Plans for a Satisfying Life. Suffice to say here that a plan has to be developed so that money is moved to Security Assets that will be secure, and separated from Wealth-creating Assets. Your Wealth-creating Assets (business, shares, property investments) are the things that will make you rich.

Your Security Assets will keep you rich and allow you to have the lifestyle you dream of and are planning for. This template allows you to fill in the numbers so that you have your own personalised plan.

You need a deliberate policy of putting aside a part of the income from your Wealth-creating Assets into your Security Assets. Your plan has to be worked out thoughtfully, at a quiet time, and then you have to *stick to it*. Do not mindlessly reinvest everything back into your Wealth-creating Assets. Always keep in mind what you are trying to do: plan the work, and then work the plan. The reasons behind this plan are:

- When things get tough (as they will from time to time) you will have some capital that you could use to take advantage of the low asset values that are around in downturns. Smart operators sit on their hands when times are good. They let the good times increase their income and wealth, but they do not go out and aggressively acquire more until things get tough. In this way they are in a position to buy more property, shares or business assets at bargain prices, which they can hold and improve while they wait for the inevitable upturn. This is the 'buy in gloom, sell in boom' syndrome—but you must have held back some capital to be able to buy when everyone else is gloomy and selling.
- You will have a fallback position, which means that if you do get caught in a 'vicious spiral' you have other assets that you can use to help you survive. Getting rich takes a number of years. You want to be set up in such a way that you can weather adverse economic conditions (such as recession), problems in your particular wealth-creating activity, and even difficult personal circumstances such as illness or other family problems. A smart wealth creator knows that some or all of these obstacles will be encountered at some time.

- The final goal of financial freedom is to have significant wealth in secure investments (Security Assets) that will generate sufficient passive income to support the lifestyle you want. You should be shifting some of the profits from your Wealth-creating Assets to Security Assets right from the beginning.
- While moving money to Security Assets from your Wealth-creating Assets may go against the grain at first, investing outside your business or property investments is a very good habit to get into. It constantly reminds you that the aim of your activities is not just to get rich, but to be in a position where you will stay rich, and have enough passive income to be able to choose how to spend your time.

In some ways, this model is simplicity itself. Certainly no-one has trouble understanding the principles—there is nothing very complicated about the idea of shifting some of your wealth outside your business, farm, property portfolio (or whatever other venture you are using to become rich). What is *not* simple is actually working the plan.

It is all too easy when you have a successful Wealth-creating Asset to instinctively plough all of the profits back into it. Not a great deal of thought goes into this—expansion automatically occurs as cash becomes available. Little thought is given to, or plans made for, other uses of the cash generated by profits.

That such action is instinctive is the problem. Ploughing back everything that you make is not a thoughtful approach; rather it is an unplanned, unexamined, unquestioned habit. Smart entrepreneurs take a much more informed, business-like approach to their wealth-creating activity. Not only is reinvesting all profits likely to be less than optimal business practice, but it is also likely to prevent you from realising your dreams of financial freedom.

The real benefit of our model of the Triangle of Financial Freedom is that it forces you to think about what you are going to do with your profits; forces you to plan to split the profits three ways: for consumption (you have to live); for the Wealth-creating Assets (you have to reinvest some of the profits); and for Security Assets (you have to diversify some of your wealth out to investments which will generate passive income).

It is this last part that most entrepreneurs miss—all their wealth is employed to make them rich; none of it to help them stay rich and become free.

The triangle helps you keep the different things that you own in different compartments (in your mind at least). It encourages you to use part of the income that you receive on an ongoing basis on things that are secure. Best of all perhaps, it reminds you why you are setting out to become rich: that it is not just money that is important but financial freedom. Money, wealth and riches are only important for the kind of life that they allow you—the kind of life you want.

Part II

Dreams, goals and plans for a bigger life

Chapter 8 | Your Dreams, goals and plans for a bigger life

Before you do anything, have a think about the why, what and how of financial freedom. Many people are tempted to rush in and start doing things before they have spent a little (or a lot of) time thinking and writing about what wealth and freedom mean to them. You need to consider your *dreams* (why do you want wealth and freedom in the first place?), your *goals* (what do you need to achieve in order to be rich and free?) and your *plans* (how are you going to achieve your goals for wealth and freedom?).

The order of these three things is important: the dream or vision leads to your being able to set goals, which in turn means that you can make plans. The dream is the most important thing—it must come first. If you don't have a dream of the life you want you will find financial freedom very hard to achieve; there will be no compelling vision to pull you forward and support your efforts. Dreams are about love (the life you love, the people you love) and love is the most motivating emotion of all. Finding this dream and defining it clearly is often the hardest part of the planning process, and in lots of cases takes the most time. However, there is little point in setting goals and making plans until you know what life you want and have a vision of a better future.

Once you have a picture that is clear and strong, you can set goals. Then you can make plans that will achieve these goals. These three things are the why, what and how of financial freedom.

Dreams (*why* do you want to be free?)

↓

Goals (*what* has to be achieved for wealth and freedom?)

↓

Plans (*how* will you become rich and free?)

You must also recognise that your road to financial freedom will be a long one; you will have to plan to take years to achieve it (few people will take less than ten years).

It may be that ten years or more seems too long a time. It may be that you will find it too hard to take the necessary risks and make the necessary sacrifices for something that is so far off it does not seem real. The people who achieve financial freedom overcome these potential disincentives by always keeping in mind their dream of the life they want. Only a very clear vision of a bright and exciting future will be powerful enough to keep you going to achieve what you want. Only a clear dream will give you the energy and stickability you will need to get the life you want.

Chapter 9 | The dream's the thing!

In defining your dream (the *why* of your financial freedom), remember that numbers (things like having $2 million in ten years, for example) are your goals. Numbers are your targets. They are important to have and keep in mind (and on paper as well!). But numbers are only numbers—it is the vision or dream of yourself enjoying financial freedom that will really motivate you and keep you going when things get tough. Nobody gets out of bed for a number! Not many of us are motivated by a few figures written down on a piece of paper. Most of us will be motivated by a dream of having and doing what we desire, being and becoming whatever we feel we are meant to be, by a desire to make a contribution and leave something better behind, and to take care of those who we love.

What is it that your very core being is crying out for? What do you *really* want? These are hard questions. However, the answers are unlikely to be a 'seven-figure bank balance' or 'a net worth statement with lots of zeros on the end'. These things may be your goals, but they are goals to be achieved on the way to reaching your dream: perhaps it's helping your family, a life of travel, the ability to keep working forever because you own the company, going back to university to study Art History, taking a six-month creative writing course, circumnavigating Australia in your yacht or making a difference in a developing country.

Those who achieve financial freedom have a picture in their heads of what they want. They see themselves with the lifestyle that they want and what they want to accomplish when they have financial freedom. This is not really about money—it is much more powerful than that. The money affords the lifestyle, but it is the image (or dream) of the lifestyle that is really important.

Take time to clarify the dream that really moves you. Some of you will already have a clear idea of what is really and ultimately important to you, what you really love; many others will not have given it a great deal of thought. You may not be able to get a very clear picture of what you really want in life in just one quick session—it may require consideration for some weeks.

It is not enough to simply want to be 'rich'! Grasping for money, cruising the markets, looking out for the main chance, are rarely successful ways of achieving financial freedom. Those who win through are those with a picture of life in the future that is much stronger than just having a lot of money. The life that the money will give you is the real driver, rather than the money itself.

Life is not a dress rehearsal—you only get the one 'live' performance! Ask yourself: How do you want it to be? How are you going to spend the only time you have in this world? What do you want your life to be about? What do you want to do? Have? Be? Leave behind? You can have whatever you want—but you have to want it enough to do what it takes to make it happen.

It is possible that your answer to these questions is that you are not prepared to spend time doing the hard stuff, that you are not prepared to give things up now in order to have more later. In that case, keep on doing whatever it is you are doing now. There is nothing wrong with this—it is what most people do.

If you have a powerful enough, clear enough dream of what life with financial freedom would be like, of how you would spend your time and what you would do, you will make the necessary changes.

When you have that picture, try to get it down on paper. Put down the few things that are truly important to you.

Being financially free is about having the financial security and the freedom to spend your time in the areas that are most important to you. What is important is for the individual to decide—only you can decide what *you* want. Our wealth-coaching clients have talked about these sorts of dreams and images:

- sitting in the sunshine;
- travel overseas;
- peace of mind;
- independence;
- health and leisure;
- security;
- friends and family;
- spirituality and reflection;
- care of people who matter;
- putting something back;
- learning and further education;
- feelings of optimism;
- being debt-free;
- being job-free;
- doing for others;
- nice house and garden;
- recreation and hobbies; and
- writing a novel or poetry.

It is often difficult to put into words the picture you have in your mind's eye, but that should not stop you trying. Because that picture of financial freedom is so important, it needs to be very clearly and powerfully defined. This leads us to another important quality of the dream—it is not so much what it *is* as what it *does.* The vision you have must be compelling and attractive enough to drive you forward, to make you reach out and grab it. Powerful dreams are always positive.

Psychologically, human beings are motivated to move *towards* something rather than *away* from something else. In other words, a picture of yourself *enjoying freedom* rather than a notion of *not being trapped and constrained* will more readily motivate you. The brain is a wonderfully positive organ! Your dream must fill you with positive feelings every time you think about it so that you remain committed to what you have to do. While visions and pictures are not easy to describe and put in writing, try to come up with a few key words on paper that you can come back to if ever your dream starts to fade.

Too few of us take the time to *really* think about what we *truly* want in life—we are too often focused on just getting through the week, paying the next Visa bill, wishing for Friday, or hanging out for the next holiday. Many of us put more effort into purchasing a new fridge or remodelling the bathroom than we put into planning for the rest of our lives.

We firmly believe, however, that you *can* have what you want for the future—and that you *should* have what you want. Clarifying a dream for your future life is important work and not to be taken lightly. If you are unused to this kind of thinking, it can take a while to work through what is really important to you. And, of course, what matters may change over time. That is your prerogative—you can keep changing or upgrading your dream. But at any point in time, it is important to know what you are striving towards. Showing you how to do it is the easy part; the most difficult thing for most people is to be so clear about what they want—the endgame—that they always have the energy and the drive required to overcome their fears, blockages and 'buts'!

A compelling dream, a vision of what you want in your life, provides the why for getting rich and staying rich. The rest of this book will help you with the what and the how of financial freedom. Only you can provide the why. What needs to be done, and how to do it, will become clear when your dreams are clear.

Remember, wealth creation is an act of love—love of

yourself, family and others, and love of the life you want. The dream will not be about being rich itself, rather it will be about how you could live your life and direct your energies if you were financially free. Success is the achievement of worthwhile dreams. Wealth is just the vehicle for realising your dreams. It takes a lot of time and work to create this wealth, so you must make sure your dream is powerful enough to make that effort worthwhile. Becoming wealthy takes a great deal of commitment. We will continue to refer to your dream throughout this book as it provides the overall objective for becoming and staying financially free. Consider the real cost of not having a dream—that which *might have been* in your life never gets a chance.

Knockers will tell you that you don't have to be wealthy to be free. It's simply not true. Unless you are irresponsible or have no-one you care about or little you wish to achieve, you need resources to pursue any of the sorts of dreams listed earlier. Someone who is wealthy can help their parents when they are old and need care, and help their children when they need it. Wealthy people have those choices—those who are not wealthy often do not. Undoubtedly, people can content themselves with very little, but it often means settling for a very constrained life. Wealth gives you choices—the ability to choose the life you want. *The financially free have bigger lives.*

Before you read on, ask yourself these questions:

- What do you really want?
- If you won a lottery, what would you do?
- What do you love?
- What do you want to achieve over your lifetime?
- If money were no obstacle, how would you spend your life?
- If you only had five years to live, what would you do?
- If you knew you were going to die soon, what regrets would you have?

- What do you want as your epitaph?
- What would you like people to say was your legacy?

Make your dreams big—small dreams have no power. Don't worry at this point about how you are going to make the dream a reality—there will be a way if you want it enough. Concentrate here on building your castle in the air; you can put in the foundations later.

Chapter 10 | Setting your goals

Setting your goals is the what of financial freedom (deciding what you are going to need to make the life of your dreams).

People who become rich and free set goals and make plans to ensure that their dream becomes a reality. The goals are numeric—they are the amounts of money that you will need to afford the lifestyle of your dreams. People who become wealthy set goals, and they put those goals in writing. No-one has ever satisfactorily explained why it is that goals that are committed to paper are achieved, but time and time again it is proved that they are.

Even when you have a compelling dream it can be very difficult to know where to start. Goals are about making the dream more concrete. The goals that you set should be numerical. For example:

- I will have a net worth of $2 million by the year 2015.
- I will have $1 million in secure investments by 2010.
- I will get a 20 per cent return on my business.
- I will buy 3 investment properties this year.

Goals have to be tailored and customised in line with each person's particular dream. You will need to set goals that will stretch you—big dreams need big goals.

The great value of numbers is that they cannot be fudged; if you put the numbers that are your goals down on a piece of paper, you cannot lie to yourself about what you meant. It is easy to wax lyrical when we just talk about our dreams, and we can easily shift our goals if we do not want to be pinned down. Having those numerical goals set down starkly in black and white gives you the determination to achieve them, because if you do not there is no doubt that you have failed. (This is why business is so wedded to numbers—numbers force people to be concrete and definite about their intentions!)

As well as your final goal, you may put in some shorter-term milestone goals, such as: by 2007 I will own my own business and it will be making $100 000 a year, or by 2005 I will own seven rental properties. Don't be too glued to these milestone goals, however, for the path to financial freedom often does not move in a perfect smooth upward line. Things are likely to be much more lumpy, with a rush of success followed by a long period of going sideways, even a decline.

It is the long-term final goal that is really important; the shorter-term goals are only there to help keep you on the right track—they act as signposts to guide you on your way and to check your progress.

Goals are important—but they are not as important as the dream that creates them. It is your vision or dream of financial freedom that will really motivate you to do what is necessary. Once you have your vision, and have set the goals that will satisfy it, you can start to make your plan for action. The plan is about getting yourself from here to there.

There are three numbers or benchmarks that are important for financial freedom. They are usually around the minimum quantities that you will need in order to achieve your dream. They run througout the book as benchmarks to remind you of what you are aiming at:

- $1 million (the *amount* you will need);
- 15 per cent (the *performance* you will need); and
- 10 years (the *time* you will take).

$1 million (The AMOUNT you will need)

This is the absolute bare minimum amount of wealth needed to be financially free—that is, your net worth has to be at least $1 million.

It is possible to be financially free with this amount, provided you do not have too much wealth tied up in your home, and have a relatively modest lifestyle. For example, someone who had a house worth $300 000 and investments of $700 000 could be financially free (as long as they did not want to spend three months skiing in St Moritz each year). An amount of $700 000 safely invested could give you enough income to enjoy financial freedom; for example, $700 000 put into industrial property at a yield of 10 per cent would give an annual income of $70 000, enough to live a modest dream.

In reality, you should be aiming for a net worth a good deal higher than this—$1 million is the least that you are likely to get away with. More invested in Security Assets will obviously give you a greater passive income.

15 per cent (The PERFORMANCE you will need)

What we are talking about here is the return that you should be looking for from the capital you put into your Wealth-creating Assets. You will not get that sort of return from your Security Assets—being much safer and less aggressive, they are likely to return nearer 5 per cent.

However, you need a higher return to make yourself wealthy. Unless you have a highly paid job and can save a lot from it, 5 per cent is simply not good enough—it will be too slow. You need a much higher return to speed up the process of growing capital. This is why few people become very wealthy with the classic diversified portfolio. A return of 15 per cent from your Wealth-creating Assets is a good benchmark to become rich. It is what makes your Wealth-creating Assets wealth creating!

The rule of 72

If you can get a return of 15 per cent, your wealth will double every 4.8 years. The rule of 72 tells us how long it will take for an investment to double if you know the return that you will get. If you divide 72 by the investment return, you will get the number of years it will take for your investment to double in value. Thus, an investment return of 10 per cent will see your wealth double in 7.2 years; a return of 15 per cent doubles it in 4.8 years; a return of 20 per cent doubles it in 3.6 years.

Note that a return of 15 per cent is the minimum you should be aiming for. Many people will look for 20 or 25 per cent. Some people try to get even greater returns than this, particularly from business enterprises. Note also that this return of 15 per cent is the *combined return* from both income and capital growth. It is the rate at which the capital you have invested is growing and compounding.

Is it possible to get that sort of return on your money? Yes, it is—but not without taking some risks. You will have to borrow (risky in itself) and the things that you have your money in will be volatile (that is, will not grow smoothly) at that sort of high rate. We can guarantee (nearly!) that if you chase returns as high as this, you will have plenty of ups and downs—and the downs will have you wondering whether you are on the right track. (We never said that this would be easy.)

Nevertheless, you *can* get a return of 15 per cent or more on your Wealth-creating Assets, and that is what you are going to have to look for. Much of the latter part of this book is concerned with showing where and how you can get these high returns.

10 years (the TIME you will take)

You should be aiming to be financially free in ten years' time, or at the very least be well on the way. Ten years may not be long enough, but aiming for any period much more than this will seem too long and be demotivating for some people. If you are now 25 years old, perhaps you will not be able to retire at 35, but you should nevertheless have the end in sight. If ten years is not long enough to complete the task, it is certainly long enough to have the foundations down and most of the building blocks in place.

Obviously, the length of time that it will take to achieve financial freedom depends on your starting point—if you already have a net worth of $500 000, financial freedom can be a lot quicker than if you are starting with $20 000. If you already have $500 000 and get 15 per cent on that money, you will have $1 million in 4.8 years, and $2 million in 9.6 years.

Using a return of 15 per cent, someone who starts with $100 000 will have $1.6 million in a little less than 20 years' time. If you have more to start with, or can get a better return over the years, you will get there a lot faster. (Someone who has $200 000 and gets a 20 per cent return will have $1.6 million in less than eleven years). If you have less than this to start with, you had better get on with it!

Working out these sorts of numbers is a critical part of goal setting. You will need to find your starting point, look at how much you can put into Wealth-creating Assets, set a return that you will aim for and then use the rule of 72 or compound interest tables to calculate where you will be in ten years.

Diagrammatically, the process of goal setting looks something like this:

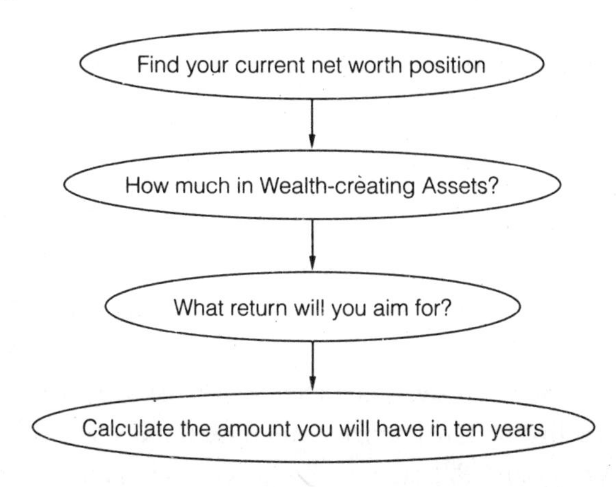

If the amount you will have in ten years is not enough, you have to go back and question some of your assumptions. In effect, you may have to play with the numbers to achieve what you want. Ask four questions:

- Can you put more of what you currently have into Wealth-creating Assets?
- Can you get a greater return than 15 per cent?
- Are you sure that the final figure is not enough to let you live your dream?
- Perhaps you will have to wait longer than ten years for financial freedom?

The numbers need to be looked at, each in turn, and looked at again until you have a reasonable time period in which to achieve your goal.

A ten-year timeframe to achieve financial freedom is not at all unreasonable. It may sound impossibly long for some people, but it does mean that a 40-year-old will be free at 50 years old (and, yes, there is still life at 50). Some will achieve it much quicker than this. Those in business or property development, and some other activities, can probably look to less than ten years.

Your aim should be to achieve financial freedom within ten years because it is difficult to plan further ahead than this. Perhaps more importantly, it is hard to maintain enthusiasm and motivation if the time period seems too long. If you are 35 years old now, it is hard to imagine yourself at 50 or 55 years. It is hard to imagine or envision where you will be or what you will be like in, say, 20 years, and so your timeframe needs to be less than that period.

You will need to set goals that work for your dream. This can take a bit of hard work and debate. It's worth it. Your mind loves goals! When you have set your goals your mind will be focused firmly on them—all the time. Your goals should be very powerful—and the fewer and clearer the better!

Chapter 11 | The Get Rich, Stay Rich plan

The plan that we use (the how of financial freedom) is our Get Rich, Stay Rich triangle. This basic format that we use with all our wealth-coaching clients allows us (and the client) to conceptualise things, to put language around what we are trying to do, to put labels on the various things that clients have and are doing. It puts the various things that people own, or plan to own, in different compartments, and makes sure that they have the right balance between them. Perhaps the best thing about this format or template is that it suits everyone—we have not yet found anyone whose financial plan cannot be put into this basic model.

To get rich, you only need assets that will make you money. However, to get rich and stay rich, you need to break down your finances into three parts. Even while you are getting rich, you should not have everything in high-performance Wealth-creating Assets. You need to hold some assets or money aside as a fallback in case of adversity, and to remind you that the endgame is having a lot of wealth in secure assets which will provide passive income. To get rich and stay rich you need these three things:

- Wealth-creating Assets;
- Security Assets; and
- Income.

Each of these is set in a box or compartment of the model. To understand the process involved in the Get Rich, Stay Rich triangle, you should think of them as separate things. Nevertheless, although they are separate, they inter-relate and interact.

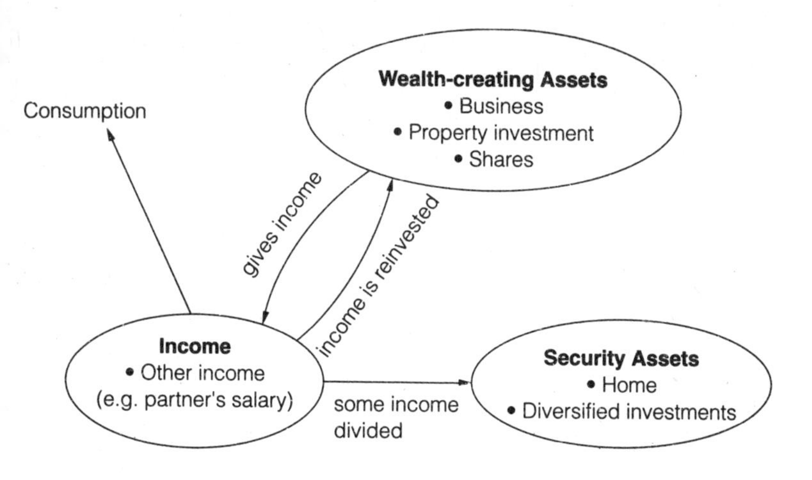

We explain each one briefly here (there is much more detail in later chapters).

Wealth-creating Assets

These are the things that will make you wealthy, the things that you put your money into with the intention of getting at least a 15 per cent per annum return. They are aggressive assets: high performance and high risk. They are the opposite of the diversified portfolio investments—they cannot be diversified if they are to achieve a 15 per cent return (or more).

There are really only three things that will make you this sort of return: a business; property investment or development; and shares.

You do not get high returns from just anything in these categories. Not all business or property investments or shares will give you the growth that you need to get rich. You also need to know how to go into whichever you choose. However, these are the only three categories that are able to give a high enough return to grow your wealth to financial freedom.

We have already said that the ownership of these kinds of things is risky: your own business is inherently risky (many do not last more than five years); property is risky because it has high borrowings; and shares are volatile, going up and down, and sometimes only down.

The risks associated with owning these things mean that you cannot own only these things and expect to have financial freedom; you will not have financial security while you own only these. You may have great wealth, but the risks that are inherent in Wealth-creating Assets mean that you cannot relax and call yourself free.

Thus, while these things will help you on the way to becoming rich, they are not the endgame in themselves. You need to have more secure investments, ones that are unassailable.

Security Assets

In this box are the assets that are unassailable. This is where you may keep your house and a diversified portfolio of investments. This part of the structure should have no (or at least very little) borrowings.

When you first start off towards financial freedom, you will have very little in the Security Assets compartment. Clearly, you have to get as much of your capital working as hard as possible in your Wealth-creating Assets, getting those high returns. If you put a lot into Security Assets, too much of your wealth will be under-performing to make you rich in the time required. Early on, most of your capital should be in Wealth-creating Assets, the idea being to transfer some of it progressively into Security Assets.

Nevertheless, right from the start you should start to develop Security Assets, even though there may not be much at first. You should start to develop them at the beginning for two reasons:

- **Increasing your Security Assets teaches you the habit of putting some money away** Doing so should continue to remind you what the *final* goal is: to have everything, all of your wealth, in these sorts of assets.
- **They will give you some fallback funds if things should go wrong** Remember that ploughing everything back into your Wealth-creating Assets means that you are playing double or quits with the stakes getting higher and higher, and one bad mistake could see you out of the game. Having some assets put aside allows you to prop up your Wealth-creating Assets during a lean period, or to start again if the worst happens. You will have the means to get back in the game.

We know it is tempting to keeping putting everything into your Wealth-creating Assets, especially when you are doing well there. Keep telling yourself: the biggest enemy of the entrepreneur is over-optimism. Early success leads many people to think that the game is easy and that everything they touch turns to gold. *This is an illusion.* You are not perfect, you are not a god—you will make mistakes. You may have been successful first off, but that does not make you invulnerable forever. Get the Security Assets started immediately, even if you only put a little in at the beginning. Over time you can divert more into it, paying off the home loan first, and then developing that diversified portfolio.

This will necessarily slow you down a little on your road to riches. The things in the Security Assets compartment will not get the returns that your Wealth-creating Assets will get (expect to get 5 per cent here, rather than 15 per cent). Nevertheless, this is a very positive step towards financial freedom. Getting rich is only half of the story—staying rich is the other half. You need to find a balance from the beginning.

Assets in the Security compartment should preferably be owned by an entity quite separate from everything else you do—possibly some kind of trust. The idea is to make your Security

Assets unassailable if things go wrong. If they are quarantined off from your other activities, they will still be yours if everything else collapses around you.

Income

Your income will come from one or more of three sources:

1. **Your Wealth-creating Assets** This may be a business and in some cases may be your only source of income (at the beginning anyway).
2. **Your Security Assets** This is likely to be quite small at the start. All income generated from this area should be reinvested back into it, at least until you start to need the passive income it generates to enjoy your freedom.
3. **Your job or your partner's job.**

Some people, especially those who are quite advanced in their quest for financial freedom, may get income from all three sources (although those people can ignore the income from Security Assets and simply reinvest it).

The next big part of the plan is to decide what you are going to do with your income. This needs to be split three ways:

- **Consumption** You have to live: pay for the groceries, rent or mortgage on the house, power, telephone, etc. The more you spend in this area, the less you will have for the other two things. (There is a lot more on consumption in Part III.)
- **Wealth-creating Assets** This area is likely to take the lion's share of income after consumption is allowed for (in the early days at least). You will want to put as much spare income as possible into this area: to buy more properties or shares or to fund growth in the business. You want to use the compounding

effect as much as possible in the area that is growing your wealth and making you rich.
- **Security Assets** Some small portion of your spare income at the beginning should be put here. Initially, when your income is small and need for growth is high, the percentage will be small—perhaps only 5 per cent. Later on you will divert more, until in perhaps ten years' time, when you are fully focused on freedom rather than wealth creation, all spare income is siphoned off to Security Assets.

Planning to allocate your money like this is critical to your chances of reaching financial freedom. If you do not plan to divide your income, you may spend it mindlessly—you could become rich, but you probably will not stay rich. Make a deliberate plan to split your income and set up automatic payments through your bank account.

Updating the Get Rich, Stay Rich triangle

Filling in the numbers and writing them into the Get Rich, Stay Rich triangle needs to be done for different time periods. We recommend you do a one-year, three-year, five-year and ten-year plan. For each plan, you will need to work out:

- How much income you will have.
- How much consumption you must allow (you will have to do a personal budget).
- How much will go into Security Assets.
- How much will be reinvested in Wealth-creating Assets.
- How much there will be in Security Assets and in Wealth-creating Assets.

You will have to work through these numbers on separate pieces of paper and maybe have separate files for each. Once you are confident that they all fit together properly, you can put them into the Get Rich, Stay Rich triangles. This will mean that each plan (for each time period) is on one piece of paper and so will be easy to refer to and change when the need arises.

Chapter 12 | Keeping it in proportion

A question we are often asked is: What proportions should be allocated to Security Assets and to Wealth-creating Assets?

It is not an easy question to answer, as there is no magic formula for these percentages. Everybody has a different position; everybody is in a different age or stage. Ultimately, how this is arranged is a matter of judgment.

Along the spectrum of people heading for financial freedom, from the young person just starting out to the older person who already has a high net worth, the proportions vary with circumstances.

- **Older high net worth person** This person should be putting nearly everything in Security Assets. The position of financial freedom is only attained when there is enough passive income from safe investments to live your dreams. This person should be putting all income into Security Assets and should be thinking about cashing up Wealth-creating Assets (selling the business or properties) to enjoy the freedom that was dreamed of. This person already has *enough* to be free and should now be concentrating not on creating wealth, but on starting to enjoy it.
- **Younger low net worth person** This person still has to get rich so does not yet have the same concerns about staying rich. Most of this person's wealth should be in Wealth-creating Assets. Nevertheless, a start should be made on Security Assets and a small percentage of income should be going to increase the home's mortgage payments or into a diversified portfolio. While this may not be much at the beginning it is a start and can (and should) be increased later. Making a start has the

effect of reminding this person about the endgame and creates the habit of siphoning money off into secure areas.

The chances are you fit somewhere in between these two examples. The proportions that you choose are individual to you. We have found people in their forties with valuable homes who have virtually nothing in Wealth-creating Assets. To become rich they need to take capital from their house (perhaps by selling it or mortgaging it) and get it working harder in high-return areas. We have found others with very valuable businesses, farms and properties, people who already have enough for financial freedom, who need to shift significant amounts across into Security Assets.

Factors that need to be taken into account in working out the proportions to allocate include your age, your current net worth, the time desired to reach financial freedom, the riskiness of the things that you own and the amount of your borrowings.

It may be that you have to take dramatic steps to achieve financial freedom—sell the house or the business, slow down the growth of property or share purchases to shift more to Security Assets, slow down contributions into a super fund and go more into aggressive investments.

Look at what you own—do a net worth statement and put what you own into the appropriate compartment (see Part IV). If the proportions are not right, you can shift capital from one box to the other. There is always a way of doing this, even if it is hard (it may mean selling something). Look at the big picture of what you are trying to achieve; remind yourself of the dream. If you want financial freedom enough, you will be able to find a way to achieve the right balance.

Chapter 13 | A planning example

When anyone approaches us for wealth coaching, the first thing we always do is find their current financial position.

In the case of a particular couple working together in their own business it looked like this:

Assets:		
	House	$380 000
	Manufacturing company	$300 000
Liabilities:		
	Mortgage	$95 000
	Company debt	$120 000
	Net worth	**$465 000**
Their income was:		
	Company profit	$95 000 (after tax)
	Wife's salary	$25 000 (after tax)
	Total income	**$120 000 (after tax)**

We made three recommendations.

1. The company (a manufacturing business) should be regarded as their Wealth-Creating Asset. It was a good little business and had been running quite satisfactorily for six years in a strong market. The business had plenty of potential to grow and we undertook to help them achieve that growth.
2. The house, with its mortgage, should be regarded as a Security Asset. This part of their finances would have the repayment of the mortgage as the first priority.
3. The income should be divided like this:

Consumption	$40 000
Reinvested in the business	$65 000
Security Assets	$15 000

The income that was to go to Security Assets would be used to accelerate the repayment of the mortgage.

Diagrammatically our recommedation looked like this:

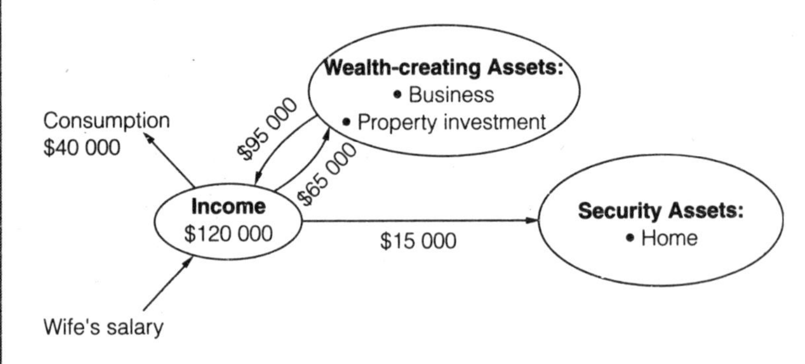

Note that although the diagram only shows $15 000 going to the Security Asset, part of the money for consumption was already going there as they had a mortgage over 20 years on which they were paying $900 a month. Thus, of the $40 000 p.a. for consumption, around $10 000 p.a. was already going to the house.

We further agreed that for the next three years, the income would be split to Security Assets and to the business in the same proportions—that is, the proportion of the profit that the business retained would be maintained as it grew, as would the amounts to the Security Assets. However, the amount for consumption for the next three years would remain at $40 000. This was actually a major decision that would have far-reaching (and beneficial) consequences. Most people spend more as their income rises—it seems a basic rule of life that consumption increases at a rate directly proportional to increases in income. Agreeing to limit spending for three years would see significantly more income go back into the business and to Security Assets than would otherwise be the case.

Automatic payments were set up with the bank so that the plan would be easy to maintain. Our major coaching role was to help with the business as well as ensuring that the couple stuck to their plan for dividing their income. This was harder than it sounds, as the business had been taking all of the couple's spare cash since it had been set up six years earlier. We had to ensure not only that there was a plan but also that there was the discipline and skills required to stick to the plan. Automatic payments are often a good way of ensuring this.

This is a very simple example. Some people's affairs are much more complicated. Nevertheless, it is a good example of the use of the model to conceptualise how things can be planned and arranged. The model, and the plan that resulted, allowed this couple to see what they were doing and gave them a sense of purpose. They could now talk about what they were doing and see where they were heading. The model gave them a framework that allowed them to easily see the consequences of not sticking to it (either by over-consuming or putting too much back into the business). The couple had ownership of the plan, shared the dream and had a common language to talk about their goals and progress.

Part III

Smart use of income

Chapter 14 | What will you do with your income?

We now need to look at the income that you have. This means doing a budget (dreaded word!). All successful enterprises have a business plan. At the heart of that plan is a budget. Your enterprise is no different—your plan must have a budget too.

The important thing is not the amount of money you make—it's what you keep that counts. This means having a surplus, your income exceeding expenditure. We always smile when people measure the size and success of their businesses by their sales revenue. We smile because sales revenue, no matter how big, is irrelevant if there is no surplus after costs are met. It is the same with your personal affairs—your income is not important, it is what is left over to be invested that matters.

The first part of any budget is to look at what income is coming in. This could come from a number of sources:

- your job;
- your partner's income;
- your Wealth-creating Assets (business, farm, share dividends, property rentals, etc.); and
- your Security Assets (although any income generated here will usually be ignored as it should be reinvested in Security Assets).

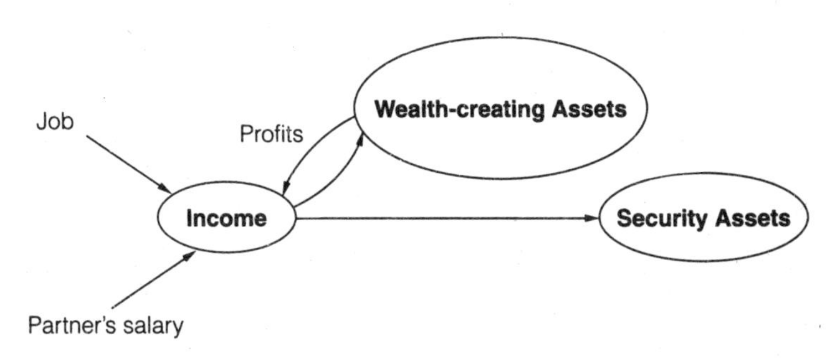

Add up all the income you are receiving. Before you do anything else, see if you can maximise that income: are the rents on your properties at full market; have you or your partner asked for a raise in salary lately; are you sure your business is as profitable as possible? There is a tendency for people to only think about expenditure only when they are budgeting. However, just as in a business, the income side is at least as important as the expenditure side. You should always be looking for ways to drive up income.

When you are sure of your total income, you need to allocate it to three areas:

- consumption;
- Wealth-creating Assets; and
- Security Assets.

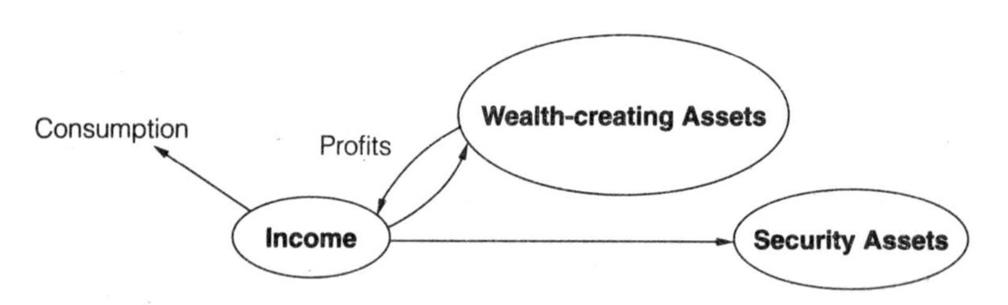

The splitting of income between Wealth-creating Assets and Security Assets is a major theme of this book. It is a key part of your plan and is dealt with in detail later.

Most of this section is concerned with consumption. Taking control of your consumption, what you spend on yourself now, is one of the key things to do. A dollar saved today is a dollar that can be invested and turned into two dollars (or five dollars) tomorrow. (Well, perhaps not quite that quickly!)

For the future you want, you will have to give up something today.

Chapter 15 | Stop your mindless spending

Stopping any mindless spending (and thus learning to live below your means) is where the going gets tough for a lot of people. To achieve financial freedom you will have to cut your consumption, the amount that you spend on things. It is tough because there are great and powerful forces out there telling you to do just the opposite. We are accustomed to living up to, and even living beyond, our means. We consume more of everything than we need, or even really want in some cases. Most people are overspending; many of us are over-eating, over-dressing, and so on! Every business in the land, backed by huge marketing budgets, is telling you to spend, spend, spend.

You will have to resist a lot of this. You have to stop being like most people; you have to stop mindless spending. Mindless spending is buying things that you do not need, or buying things that give you no real pleasure. Mindless spending is buying things that you have never really *thought* about buying, where your mind has not been involved in the decision to buy. In large part, mindless spending is buying things to make you look good in the eyes of others; in other words, it is ego-spending, buying things through emotion rather than thought. To achieve financial freedom you have to cut this, be your own person with your own aims, which have nothing to do with how you appear to others. Living below your means (rather than *above* your means) is a key step in becoming rich and financially free.

Every dollar that you spend is a dollar further away from your dream and your goals. In fact, it is worse: the dollar that is spent is gone; the dollar that goes into Wealth-creating Assets remains and grows. You need to be thinking about cutting the spending (money that immediately disappears for ever), and increasing the money that goes into your Wealth-creating Assets (money that is likely to earn you a 15 per cent return).

We tell our clients to think about two things.

Imagine you are spending shares, not money

Before you spend money on something, imagine that you are not spending dollars but GPG shares. (GPG is a pet company of ours that has performed extremely well for its shareholders for a decade.) If the currency you are spending is GPG shares (or some other high-performance Wealth-creating Asset), that means that forgoing that suit for $800 gains you equivalent value in GPG shares. Owning the GPG shares now will be better than owning the suit, but in 20 years' time it will be *far* better—the suit will have long gone to be a duster-rag, but if the GPG shares have grown at 20% p.a., they will be worth over $30 000. (You should be able to buy a few suits with that!)

Now, we are not saying do not buy a suit (or anything else, for that matter). What we are saying is think about the cost, not just in dollars today, but in dollars in the future. The 'real' cost of your spending is the future value of the dollars you are spending today if they had instead been invested well. There is a very real benefit in forgoing something today for a better tomorrow. The ability to delay gratification is a hallmark of successful individuals in all areas of life. The success here is achieving your dream of financial freedom.

Changing your currency to GPG shares (or some other proxy that is meaningful to you) is a good way of recognising the real cost of unnecessary expenditure. That cost is primarily what you could otherwise have in the future. The only thing that you need to be careful of is taking it too far, and ending up mean and miserable and no fun to be around. Which leads us to the second thing.

Make your spending count

By all means spend money, but make your spending count. Your spending should be 'mindful'. The latest pitch from David Jones or Michael Hill Jewellers should not dictate what you spend. These are companies that maybe you should perhaps *own* through the share market, rather than have them own your credit card! Buy quality things that will give you great pleasure. Buy only things that you really need. Think before you buy rather than buying on impulse because some slick marketing has pushed a product at you. Having a spending plan is a good way to beat the latest pitch from a retailer.

Mindful spending means buying what *you* want, not what you are *told* you want. If you get a lot of pleasure from owning a nice car, you might decide that having one is worthwhile. Do not buy a nice car because that is what others expect. Indulge yourself with things that make you happy, not things that are designed to make you look good. This is a great time to revisit your dream and vision for the future. Many of the things we spend money on do not take us in the direction of our dreams; in fact they take us away. It is much easier to bypass the temptation of mindless expenditure if you are clear about what you *really* want—you can then distinguish easily between the big things that matter, and the trivia that does not.

•

A key part of anyone's plan for wealth is a budget. Some people find this a horrible, negative-sounding word with connotations of scrimping and saving and living a poor life. There is no reason why it should be that bad, but there *is* a price to be paid for financial freedom, and a reduction of consumption is a part of that price.

Constructing a budget and then living to that budget is an important part of your plan for financial freedom. This is especially true for those starting off—making those first few steps, developing a little bit of wealth to get things going, is the greatest hurdle. Everyone says that the first $1 million is the hardest (we have heard people say that their first $1 billion was their hardest, but we'll have to take their word on that!). The comment, however, is just as true for the first $100 000, or even the first $10 000.

If you are starting with next to nothing, your first investments can only really come from reduced consumption. If you are starting with not very much, reducing consumption will accelerate the process. Many people could become financially free just by spending less and investing the remaining money well. We have seen clients 'save' thousand of dollars *per month* from their budgets and develop an impressive investment portfolio within a year! Living below your means becomes a new habit very quickly—and a very rewarding one when you see the resulting assets accumulate.

The wealthy people we coach are not mean. They are, in fact, nearly always generous. However, almost all of them are very mindful spenders. They know what they want and they have what they want. But they do not have what they do not need; they are quite happy to go without if they are not getting the full measure of enjoyment for each dollar spent.

Switch from mindless spending to mindful spending so that you get what you want.

Chapter

16 | Your house and consumption

Your house will not make you rich and does not belong in the Wealth-creating Assets box. The growth in value of houses in general is unlikely to approach 15% p.a. long term, even though it might in some areas over short periods of time. Your house generally belongs in the Security Assets box.

However, for some people (quite a lot in our experience) the house partly fits into consumption. This is much worse than it being a Security Asset.

There are two groups of people for whom the house ceases to be a Security Asset but becomes a drain on finance.

First are the people who spend a great deal of money on their houses, a lot more than what they budget for, and in a lot of cases much more than they ever realise they are spending. Little things, extras for the garden, redecoration, all add up. The big things (new kitchen, additions and alterations) are a bigger drain (and represent a lot of GPG shares), even though they do not come along very often. These things often do not add their full value to the worth of the house, and thus become consumption rather than adding to the amount of your Security Assets. As with all consumption, you can spend this money on your house if you want, but you must realise that there is a cost.

Be *mindful* of that cost.

The second way that a house is a drain on the finances and becomes part of consumption, is when you own a house that is really too big and too valuable for your needs. People aiming for financial freedom cannot afford to have too much tied up in their house, not in the early days at least. When someone buys a house valued at the top of the market in a particular area, it has ceased to become accommodation—some other thought process has come into play. They may think that they are investing in property but really they may be looking for the 'right' address to impress family and friends. Even if they are taking great pleasure from their home, very often they have bought because they can 'afford' the mortgage repayments and have not really thought about whether such a house is the best place for their money. In effect they are living beyond their means, paying for their excesses either by putting too much capital into the house at the start (and therefore forgoing better Wealth-creating Assets) or by carrying a big mortgage (and paying through the nose for it).

This may not be a good strategy even for those who are not looking for financial freedom, because all their money is in just one 'investment'. It is most certainly not a good strategy for those who are looking for financial freedom, as a large part of their capital is tied up in one asset that is not going to create wealth. Remember always, it is not just the capital that is used to buy the house that is spent, but the often quite substantial mortgage repayments divert cash which could be better employed elsewhere. Do some numbers: have a look at where you would be if the mortgage payments were greatly reduced, or even eliminated, and that money went into your Wealth-creating Assets instead.

That expensive house certainly provides somewhere to live (and you need that), but beyond a certain level of value there is a component that is solely for pleasure or ego and so is really consumption. If that expensive house is what you really want, have it. However, it is hard to have both that house and financial freedom—you probably can't.

Those who are serious about financial freedom will delay the purchase of that big expensive house until they have made it—it is often one of the rewards. There are some who will not buy a house at all and rent instead. If you do decide to own rather than rent and you are serious about financial freedom, you will own something quite modest and get your money working. Many very wealthy people, those who have already made it, live in relatively modest homes. Those wealthy people who do have beautiful homes generally delayed that purchase until they had created their wealth—buying an expensive home did not make them wealthy!

Look hard at your house and decide how well it fits with your plans for financial freedom. For a lot of people it can provide the capital they need to put into their Wealth-creating Assets to really get started. A lovely house may be your aspiration—but you should aspire to it rather than have it now. Defer the gratification of having the great house until you have made it to financial freedom—and then *you* will own it, not the bank.

Peter and Sarah had a problem—a lack of capital for their property development business. They owned their own home and both worked full time, but they also bought houses which they did up and sold. Sometimes they would live in the house they were doing up for a few months; at other times it was a second house, which they would rent out.

For the purpose of demonstration, let's say their net worth was:

Assets		
	Home	$650 000
	Do-up property	$150 000
		$800 000
Liabilities		
	Mortgage on do-up	$60 000
Net worth:		**$740 000**

Peter and Sarah had no shortage of opportunities; there were plenty of houses to buy. They had a team of tradesmen they could call on, and they were well organised. Their lack was money—they did not ever want to have a mortgage on their home, but they did not have enough to buy more than one do-up at a time.

Peter and Sarah burned to be financially free; they had a vision of travel, writing and helping others.

Their problem was caused by putting too much money into their home—they had used the income from their jobs and the profits from the other do-ups to own a lot of house but not much else.

We gave Peter and Sarah three options:

1. Continue as is, and make their way *slowly* to financial freedom. (Not a starter!)
2. Mortgage their home and use the proceeds to buy more property. (Not a starter!)
3. Sell their home, buy something more modest and use the difference to buy more do-up properties.

This last option was hard (it was a nice place to live), but ultimately they could see that they had the balance wrong: too much in Security Assets (their home) and not enough in Wealth-creating Assets (do-ups). They decided to sell their home ($650 000), buy a house worth $350 000 and use the remaining $300 000 to turn over six do-up properties each year. The profit on this should be approximately $60 000 after tax. They would reinvest 70 per cent of the profits back into the property business and so increase the number of do-ups each year; the balance of their incomes would go to Security Assets in order to buy a better home in a few years' time.

Their plan was:

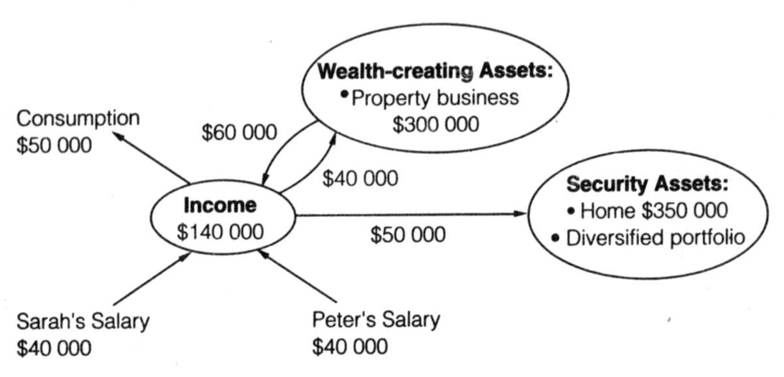

Chapter 17 | Budget tips

Doing a budget is simply making decisions about where you are going to spend your money. A budget is merely a plan for expenditure. No business would expect to succeed without a well thought-out budget, and neither should you. You will be amazed at the difference in performance when you give your own finances the same planning and monitoring as you would a business. If you are married or with a partner, you need to make these decisions together—you both have to be part of the decision-making process if the budget is going to be followed successfully.

While the word 'budget' has negative connotations for some of us, it should not really be that way. A budget is a plan for spending money. As such, it is about helping you get what you want. Few of us can have *everything* we want, so we have to prioritise. (Even the Sultan of Brunei must prioritise.) The budget process is about setting those priorities, working out what things you *are* going to have and what you are *not* going to have. A budget is a plan for mindful expenditure; no budget means that your expenditure is likely to be mindless, with spending decisions made on a whim.

There are several tips that will help you plan a successful budget:

- **Budget realistically** Our most important piece of advice is not to make the budget too tight. The psychology of dieting and the psychology of budgeting are similar—both involve a plan to 'go without', to some extent. People who go on very strict diets tend to keep them for a little while (maybe a few days or a couple of weeks) but then they break, the whole diet is discarded and a binge follows. The same can happen with budgeting: you might be able to keep to a tough budget for a few months, but once you break it, you will abandon it completely and you will be back where you started. Or worse: the whole idea of budgeting is thrown out as being useless. Budgeting realistically also means budgeting for some fun! This is about your life after all. So choose carefully the items and activities that you will spend on for entertainment and recreation; again, be planful and mindful of the end game.

- **Pay yourself first** Allocate money to your Wealth-creating Assets and your Security Assets before you look at how much you will spend on consumption. In other words, you can spend what is left over after investing for financial freedom, not invest what is left over after spending! Quite simply, most people who spend first find that there is nothing left over to invest.
- **Beware of finance offers** Do not buy things simply because the finance offer attached means you can 'afford' it. Spa pools, for example, are often sold with no actual price given in the advertising—the 'price' is given as 'from $35 per week'. The idea is that because people think $35 per week is not very much and they can find that amount, they will buy it. However, there is a price, both the capital amount (likely to be several thousand dollars) as well as interest. These two add up to an awful lot of GPG shares. Finance offers are slick marketing—don't be sucked in.
- **Look first at the big items** There are an awful lot of GPG shares here too. The things that keep people poor are the large capital items like boats, cars, the house and holidays. In the final analysis it does not make that much difference which service provider you are with for your mobile phone; the amount involved is likely to be small and you can go to a lot of trouble to save a very small amount of money. Certainly,

every little bit helps, but the big things help more. Work on the big things first—do not 'major in the minors' until you have dealt with the big-ticket items.

- **Always budget from zero** This means not putting some particular expenditure in your budget just because you have always spent money in that area. Look at each item afresh and ask yourself if that is what you really want to spend your money on: is that what you really get pleasure from? This is mindful expenditure. Budgeting is a time of decision making—how you will live your life will determine that budget, and vice versa. This section is about changing your consumption, which will probably mean changing your lifestyle to some extent. Scrutinise everything, asking whether you want to do that or need to do it.

The major spending categories are:

- housing (rates or rent, maintenance, garden costs, etc.);
- debt repayment;
- groceries (including alcohol);
- transport;
- children (child care, school fees, uniforms, etc.);
- utilities (gas, electricity, phones);
- insurance;
- clothing;
- grooming (hair care, make-up, etc.);
- medical;
- holidays;
- entertainment (movies, nights out, shows, etc.); and
- sundries (gifts, appliance replacement, etc.).

Chapter 18 | Monitor, monitor, monitor

Most of us do not really know what we spend our money on—few of us ever analyse and categorise our consumption. One of the first things we do with some of our clients is get them to carry a notebook and write down every cent they spend so that they know where their money is really going. This provides a very good reality check for the budgeting process.

One of the mantras of business is that 'you cannot manage that which you cannot measure'. The same is true for your consumption. At the end of each week or month, you and your partner need to identify what has been spent against each budget category. This should be easy to do using credit card records and cheque butts. Cash is harder to account for, but more about that later. A few months of this practice will make you both highly informed about what you are actually doing with your money and where it goes. You may even need to adjust your budget in the light of the information you now have. It is your choice. Some budgets need to be revised up, some down. After all, you need a budget you can live with, that delivers on your agreed dreams, and that allocates your spending where you really want it to go.

Your budget provides you not only with a plan for what you *intend* to spend in every category, but also a way of monitoring what you actually *do* spend. It can give you an accurate record of money in and money out. Some of our clients have been faced with some horrible truths once they started to monitor their actual expenditure! Who could have believed that so much money could be 'mindlessly' spent on takeaways, toys, fines, parking, bank fees and ATM withdrawals—thousands of GPG shares each year!

Many of our clients have been mystified regarding their disposal of cash. Nowadays it is very easy to withdraw cash from an ATM and you will have records of your withdrawals. But what happens to the cash once it's in your pocket? We have found that this is an area where people can make huge changes without too much pain. First, find out what happens to your cash by recording every piece of expenditure as you go. The notebook is very useful for this. The coins for parking, the ice cream at the garage, the cups of coffee—these all add up. You need to account for every cent until you get a clear picture of what is happening. We have found that many clients cannot account for over half of their cash spending until they start keeping meticulous records. Once you have done this for a few weeks or months you will never be so mindless with cash again! When you know where the money is going you can decide whether you are getting good value. Again, it is your choice. We never tell clients what to spend their money on—you must make those decisions in the light of your dream for financial freedom and your stated goals.

We know that this feels tedious or silly or both at first. However, imagine yourself on an investigation that will help you find several thousand dollars a year—money that you get to keep! Most people find that highly motivating. Just as with dieting, once new habits have been formed you won't need such detailed routines.

A further word on cash. While it is harder to track and monitor, we are great advocates of managing expenditure through cash. Credit cards and EFTPOS cards are smart and convenient—but our observation is that many people use them to disconnect themselves from the understanding of the amount they are consuming. It is so much easier to spend on a plastic card—it does not feel like real money. But it is! Credit card bills and bank statements come as a shock every month. Reverting to 'old-fashioned' cash may make you much more mindful—there is something very real about handing over a sheaf of $20 notes for the groceries!

Credit cards are very useful, if much abused. They are a great tool to help delay the payment of bills, and so giving you up to six weeks' free credit. They are also a very inviting way to encourage you to buy things that are not in your plan. If you have the discipline to buy only as planned and to pay the credit card bill in full every month, then a card works well. Otherwise they are a disaster, both in encouraging you to blow the budget and in the horrendous interest charges you incur unless you pay the full bill each month. We advise our clients to keep a credit card for 'emergencies'—unplanned events that require unplanned expenditure (or perhaps a really good property or business deal that you are $10 000 short on, when money from a card means you can do the deal).

If you do not have the plans and discipline that are required you should think about getting rid of your credit cards. After all, you wouldn't carry a block of chocolate around with you if you were on a diet!

Find out what you are spending your money on—go on a hunt. The wonderful thing about this is that when you hunt down some money that you are not spending and not getting good value from, you get to keep it!

Chapter 19 | Four things that boost your ego but deflate your wealth

These are:

- houses;
- cars;
- holidays; and
- hobbies.

These four things can keep you poor. They are the big items on which most of our money goes; we all have them to a greater or lesser extent. They are the areas where you can make the most savings.

Interestingly, people tend to buy these things more on the basis of ego than anything else. Much of the purchase decision is based on how it will look to other people. Less of the purchase decision is based on what *you* actually want, and whether you want it so much that you are prepared to spend so heavily on it. Will Rogers famously said, 'Too many people spend money they haven't earned, to buy things they don't want, to impress people they don't like.'

Think about how these four things are sold and marketed: they are usually pitched in a completely emotional way, an appeal straight to your feelings. They are often sold aspirationally—that is, as the kind of life that you might aspire to, or the way that you might want other people to see you. Your aspirations may be to have these things—but you should keep them as aspirations, things to have in future. To do that you will need to resist the slick marketing that companies use to get you to have them now. Have a think about that marketing.

Houses are sold with pitches like: 'imagine yourself sitting on the deck with a glass of wine watching the sun go down', or 'a good address for the discerning buyer'. People so often buy more house than they really need or, if they are wanting to become rich, more house than they can afford. Sure, you need somewhere to live, but beware of tying up too much capital in the house.

Cars are sold showing sleek and shiny people having fun in sleek and shiny metal. They are represented as the good things in life, and the underlying message is that if you buy this car people will respect and admire you, and life will be a lot of fun. In fact TV ads hardly show the car they are selling at all! They show people, the kind of people that you are meant to aspire to be. Again, you need transport, but think about how much you are spending to get yourself from one place to the other, and how much to make yourself feel and look good.

Holidays are sold with golden people on golden beaches having purple and pink drinks with little umbrellas sticking out of them. Again the message is to picture yourself here (and then you can tell your friends all about it when you get back).

We are not saying that you should not have any of these things. Rather, we are saying that you should have them only if that is what you *truly* want. Have them for yourself by all means—but do not have them for your ego and for keeping up appearances. Understand the cost of things; not just the cost in today's dollars, but the cost of the future wealth you are giving up.

Most people who are on the road to financial freedom will not bother with these things—the game is much more exciting than any flash car or holiday is ever likely to be. People in the know are aware of the future value of the money that they save and invest from not spending it on what the herd wants.

The ads for these things are aspirational—the kind of life that we all want to have. The thing they are really pushing, however, is that you can have that kind of life right now. (Just buy our car/house/holiday.) If you are really serious about financial freedom you will know that you cannot have it now—you have to defer it. That's okay because you know that you will have that kind of life (or a better one) permanently at some point in the future, and with your own money, not a finance company's money.

These things break the budget and wreck your plans. You have to resist them. They tie up so much money that the couple of dollars saved on the power or telephone bill pales to insignificance by comparison. You can make major savings on the house you live in, the car you drive and the holidays you have—savings that can go straight into Wealth-creating Assets and take you nearer to financial freedom.

Chapter 20 | Look at what you have now

As part of the wealth-creating process you have to make decisions about what you will spend your income on. You also need to think about the things that you already own.

Some of the things you own now can be converted to cash, and from cash can be converted to Wealth-creating Assets. They are things like cars, your house, boats, caravans, antiques, spa pool and so on. The house is the biggest item that you should reconsider. There is often plenty of scope here to free up capital that can be used to make you rich. However, there is also a lot of scope to convert other things into Wealth-creating Assets—they can represent a lot of GPG shares!

If such things as your car, boat, caravan or whatever give you great pleasure, you should keep and enjoy them. If your dream of financial freedom is more powerful, perhaps you should sell them. The money that you get from them can be very effectively used to advance your goals and dreams.

A client of ours illustrates this well. He was a 40-year-old property developer, fairly new to the game. About six months before we met him, he had bought a $40 000 second-hand BMW. It looked a nice little car, and he thought it presented the right image—an image to which he was aspiring but was still quite a long way from achieving.

Our client's biggest problem was lack of capital. He was adamant that there were dozens of very profitable opportunities out there, but he could not fund them all. He had no doubt that he could get a return of 25% p.a. on any capital he could get hold of.

He was sure that he could cash up the car for $35 000 (even though it was now third-hand). Our solution was obvious: sell the car for $35 000 and buy something a bit more modest (but still nice enough) for $12 000. The balance ($23 000) would fund another property development (and then another, and another). If our client could really get 25 per cent on his money for the next ten years, that $23 000 would become $214 000.

Have a look at what you have which does not give you as much pleasure as your quest for financial freedom. It may be a car, boat, caravan or even your excessive house. If you can sell some of them (even if you have to replace them with a cheaper model), you can free up some cash. Think about the cost of owning these things. Most particularly, think about the future value. Remember that if you can get 15 per cent on your money, it will double every 4.8 years.

Many people can look through what they own and find quite large amounts of money in things that they do not really want—or at least do not want as much as they want financial freedom. If you can free up $20 000 by selling some things (downgrade the car, sell the boat or caravan) and forgo others (expensive holidays, adding on a new deck to the house), the future value of $20 000 at 15 per cent is $327 000 in 20 years' time. That is a third of the way to your minimum goal.

Certainly you may be giving some things up now, but the main cost in owning them is what their future value will be. Giving things up is a pain—but the ultimate benefits make it worth paying the cost. This pain is the hard stuff (just like eating a live frog). But if you want financial freedom, the sooner you do it, the better off you will be.

Part IV

Start from here

Chapter 21 | What are you worth?

After you have defined your dreams and set your plans (including creating a budget), the next thing you need to do is set out where you are now. This means looking at what you are worth and the types of things you have your money in—in other words, doing a net worth statement.

A net worth statement is an easy enough idea, and simple enough to do. A net worth statement means writing down what you own (your assets) and deducting what you owe (your liabilities). All you are doing is adding up the pluses and subtracting the minuses to find out how much capital you have. Here is a simple example.

Assets (+)			
	House	$210 000	
	Shares	$20 000	
	Investment property	$150 000	
	Car	$30 000	
			$410 000
Liabilities (–)			
	House mortgage	($60 000)	
	Investment property mortgage	($140 000)	
	Car hire purchase	($15 000)	
	Credit card	($5000)	
			($220 000)
Net Worth			**$190 000**

Your net worth statement is a measure of how rich you are. If you sold everything and repaid all your debts, you would have that amount of cash. This tells you where you are now. You know where you want to be (that is set out in your goals). Your plan is how you are going to get there.

Everyone should do a net worth statement (even people who are not seeking financial freedom). Not only should they do one, they should do one regularly—at least once every year. Doing a regular net worth statement allows you to see your financial progress and check that you are moving in the right direction financially, that you are becoming richer rather than poorer. If that progress is not good over a long period of time, you are doing something wrong. This means changing what you do. For those who want financial freedom, it will probably mean drastic changes to what you are doing, what you own and how you are spending your money.

If you do a net worth statement regularly (each year or maybe every six months), you can graph your progress towards your goal of financial freedom. This graph of your net worth over time could look something like this:

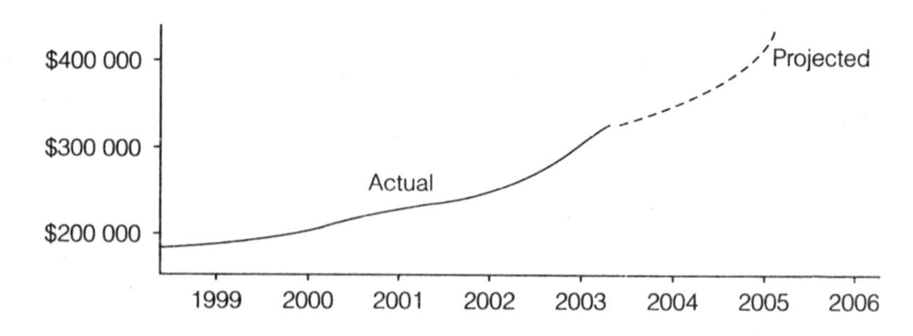

Your graph will probably be more wavy than this one, reflecting the ups and downs along the way—your progress towards financial freedom is unlikely to go in a nice smooth line.

Graphing your net worth has the very positive effect of allowing you to see how you are doing at a glance. Certainly there will be dips (and probably a few spikes as well), but the graph should, over time, run in the right direction.

Doing a net worth statement right at the beginning makes you more conscious of what is happening to your finances. You become more mindful of the impact of the decisions you are making. As you calculate your net worth consider which of your assets are actually earning you a good return and which are not. You may, for example, consider your home a wonderful asset but it isn't earning rent so, unless it is in an area which is greatly increasing in capital value, it is not a great asset. Similarly, consider which liabilities are costing you the most money. Your credit card debt will be costing you far more than your mortgage. This will give you useful information to begin planning where to reduce your liabilities.

Your net worth statement is important because it helps you to see your financial resources and how close you are to having financial freedom. Becoming rich is about building net worth—capitalism is the name of the game. You need enough net worth to give you the passive income to fulfil your dream.

Some people find when they do their first net worth statement that they already have a high net worth. Their problem is that they do not have their capital in the right things for financial freedom—it is mostly tied up in a farm, a business or a highly geared property portfolio, all of which require a lot of management. Others find that their asset mix is wrong to grow wealth; they may have a $1 million house (Security Asset) but only $50 000 in Wealth-creating Assets.

Knowing what you have to work with will help you make the connections between your dream and what you need to do with your financial resources in the future.

Your net worth statement tells you how rich you are, where you are starting from, and if you do it regularly (say annually), it measures your progress. It also tells you what you own. Now you need to put the things that you own into the categories of the model.

Chapter 22 | Applying the model to what you own

Once you have done a net worth statement, you can categorise what you own in terms of the Get Rich, Stay Rich triangle. This means deciding whether the things you own are Wealth-creating Assets or Security Assets. Categorising the things you currently own is a very important step, allowing you to see at a glance how well you have things balanced. When you see what your current allocation is you can decide whether it is right, and if it's not, make plans to re-balance by selling some things and buying others, or by using your income to start investing in the area which does not have enough. It may be that you currently have too many passive Security Assets to get the growth that is required to get rich. Conversely, you may have too much in aggressive Wealth-creating Assets and thus your task is to start transferring some of what you own into Security Assets.

Sometimes it is hard to know whether an asset is a Wealth-creating Asset or a Security Asset. The real test for classifying any particular asset centres on what sort of return the item is likely or able to give you. If your intention is to get a 15 per cent return (or more) from something, then that item is a Wealth-creating Asset; if the return is likely to be less than this, the item should be classified as a Security Asset. Another way to think of it is in terms of the degree of risk that an asset has—riskier assets (business, highly geared property or shares) belong in the Wealth-creating Asset box.

Some things will belong in neither the Wealth-creating Asset box nor the Security Asset box. These are things that are likely to fall in value and as such are really part of your consumption because they will make you poorer. Some people may list their car as an asset (which in a technical sense it is). However, the car is likely to fall in value (the ones that we buy always seem to). Assuming that you are going to keep the car, it should be categorised as consumption (it will certainly make you poorer).

The assets which most commonly pop up on people's net worth statements are:

- **The house** This is a Security Asset in most cases. The only exception to this is that small group of people who successfully buy a house, live in it for a year or so while they do it up and then sell it for a good profit. Generally, however, your house should be regarded as a Security Asset (although as shown in Chapter 16, there are people who put so much money into their houses that, to some extent at least, it should be classified as consumption). The house is such a big part of most people's net worth that there is a chapter on this coming up. It is completely wrong to think that your house will make you rich—it won't. It is a Security Asset, nothing more.
- **Superannuation funds** These are clearly Security Assets, likely to return around 5% p.a. If they are well diversified they make very good Security Assets.
- **The business** This ought to be a Wealth-creating Asset. If you are not getting a 15 per cent return in the value of the business, you would have to wonder why you own it.
- **Investment property** This may be a Wealth-creating Asset or a Security Asset depending on what and where it is, and how you are managing it. Judicious and aggressive purchasing and financing of rental property, along with good active management, can achieve a 15 per cent (or better) return. If that is your intention, put your investment property into the Wealth-creating Assets box. If, however, you make fairly ordinary purchases, do nothing to enhance the property and manage it fairly passively it should go into Security Assets.

- **Stocks and shares** These are the same as investment property—depending upon your intention, and how aggressive you are, they could go in either box. A widely spread, diversified portfolio of market leaders is probably a Security Asset; a portfolio of two or three smaller companies is probably a Wealth-creating Asset.
- **Mutual funds** Generally these are Security Assets. They are usually fairly conservatively managed and do not often show returns anything near 15 per cent. There are lots of exceptions, however. There are managed funds which have shown very high returns. We invest in the pharmaceutical/health care industries via mutual funds, some of which have given very high returns over long periods of time.

Categorising these things and labelling them lets you see what it is that you are doing now and the changes that you need to make for your future. You might eliminate (sell) or downgrade anything that is not really an 'asset' at all. Do your net worth statement and put each thing in the compartment where it belongs.

Barry and Julie were in their early sixties. Barry had run the family business for nearly forty years and still worked hard at it, despite some health problems. Julie had always run the family's finances and had over the years made some investments in property, as well as done a couple of property developments. Barry's whole life had been around the business and he did not know how to stop going into the factory every day. At Julie's insistence, a general manager had been appointed but Barry still tried to put in the hours, believing that if he left the business for long it would falter.

The first thing we did was a net worth position:

Assets

House	$400 000
Business	$2 600 000

Building sites	$400 000
Property Investments	$500 000
Unit trust	$30 000
Shares	$20 000
	$3 950 000
Liabilities	
Mortgage (on vacant blocks, and property developments)	$400 000
Net Worth	**$3 550 000**

The business was profitable, making $300 000 p.a. after tax.

The first thing to do was to decide what category each asset should go in. The only difficult categorisation was the vacant blocks of land for development, and the property investments. We decided that these should go into Wealth-creating Assets as they had quite high borrowings. These, and the property investments, were together worth $900 000; the mortgage was $400 000, and so we put these into the Wealth-creating Asset category at a net value of $500 000.

Their current position looked like this:

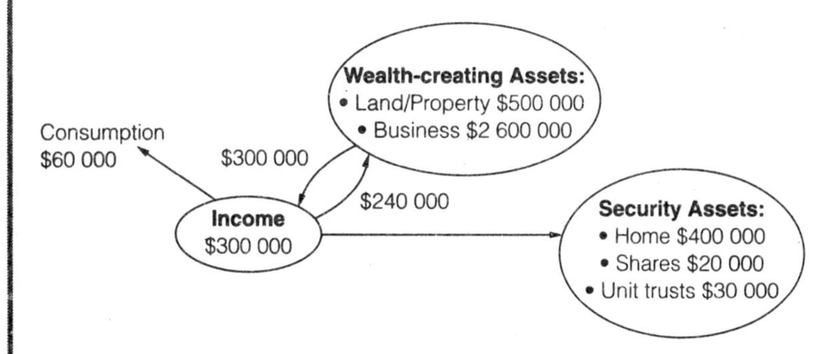

A quick glance at the triangle showed how badly balanced they were for a fairly wealthy couple in their sixties: they had $3 100 000 of their net worth in Wealth-creating Assets and only $450 000 in Security Assets. Virtually all the profits from the business were going back into it. Putting the current numbers into the model showed us quickly where the starting position was and what needed to be done.

We could now help Barry and Julie's future. The following decisions were made:

1. Half of the business would be sold to the general manager (he had been asking to buy it for ages). An arrangement would be made for the financing to help him buy a half share.
2. The proceeds from the sale of half the business would be invested in well-diversified funds.
3. With the general manager now a part-owner, Barry could relax a bit and work only when he wanted to. A board of directors would be formed with two independent directors to help govern and guide the manager.
4. A policy of paying out 66 per cent of the profits to shareholders would be adopted—half to Barry and Julie, half to the general manager (this meant each would receive $100 000 and the company would retain $100 000).
5. The vacant land would be sold (the couple did not need more big projects) and the proceeds used to retire debt. Because the property investments would now be mortgage free, they could be considered Security Assets (and would give some useful passive income).
6. More money would be budgeted for consumption for travel, holidays and so on.

When these steps were taken, the model would look like this:

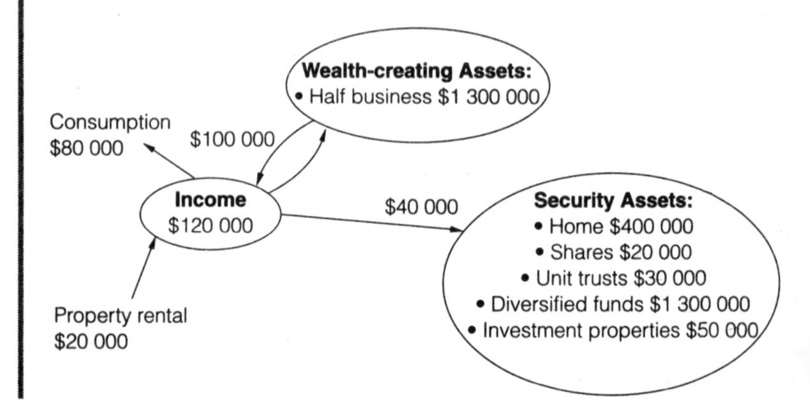

Chapter 23 | Balance is the key

When we have put what our clients currently own into the right compartments, we then set to get the right allocation and balance for achieving the vision. Usually we find that people have too much in the Security Assets box and not enough in Wealth-creating Assets to make them rich. This is particularly so when the house is the main (or only) asset. It can have so much capital tied up in it, with the mortgage taking so much of the family's income, that it is not doing anything to enhance financial freedom. Quite the opposite, in fact.

There are exceptions to this—there are a lot of people who are too heavily into Wealth-creating Assets. Business owners and property investors are the biggest group in this respect. They have everything in their businesses or property investments (except for their house) and have no plans to change from this position. This is the group we say are playing double or quits, as everything goes back into the business or buying more property.

Reallocating and balancing the things that you own can be a painful experience. It often involves selling things, a change that people are very resistant to, as you need to free up capital to get it into Wealth-creating Assets. Business owners may need to forgo some business growth and divert some profit to Security Assets; property investors may need to do the same, forgoing the purchase of another property or even selling a part of the portfolio.

None of these things are easy. Change is never easy and these sorts of big changes to what you own are amongst the hardest. There can be major emotional investments in what you have been doing, and old habits die hard.

This is where your dream or the vision is again so important. It has to be powerful enough to make you accept (even embrace) the changes that have to be made. It is easy to argue logically that the things you own and the things you have been doing have not got you to financial freedom, and you therefore have to change. But such logic is often not enough to break the emotional shackles. The only thing that will break them is the dream of something better—that vision of financial freedom to live as you wish.

At this point we bring our clients back to the dream—remind them of it, and keep reminding them. Much of our coaching is in this reallocation phase, and like all coaches we are helping people get fit and to stay motivated for the hard stuff.

And for some people, the hardest of the hard stuff involves the house.

Chapter 24 | The house might have to go

For most people their house is their biggest asset. However, once again you are not most people. If you want to achieve financial freedom, you have to be different. What you own will be different, as will what you consume. Most people have a great deal of capital in their houses, capital that keeps increasing over time as they pay off the mortgage, and pour more money into redecorating, the garden, refurbishments and alterations.

And yet we *know* that this is not the best place for your capital if you want to get rich. We know that you can do better elsewhere. Your house is unlikely to increase in value by 15 per cent. Certainly it will get some increases in its capital value, increases that are likely to approximately match (or perhaps slightly outstrip) the rate of inflation. But this is not enough to make you rich. Home ownership is a reasonable option for those who are taking the low road to a comfortable life. It is not a reasonable option for those of us who are taking the high road to financial freedom.

Our clients often tell us that they do not know where to start towards financial freedom. More particularly, they claim they have nothing to get started with. They have no capital.

When we do a net worth statement what we find is that they do have some capital—but it is all tied up in the house. Our job is then to test the strength of their desire for their dream of financial freedom: are they prepared to sell the house, rent instead, and get their capital working better? Note that renting and using the capital elsewhere is only an option when the money from the sale of the house is going into a Wealth-creating Asset. You will be better off if your money goes into something that produces 15 per cent or better; you will not be better off if it goes into something that returns 5 per cent.

For some clients the dream of financial freedom is not potent enough to make it worth selling the house. The house has strong emotional attachments, gives feelings of security and a sense of permanence. Home ownership is nearly instinctive. Both partners need to buy into the vision of financial freedom, and often one does not feel as strongly as the other (not strongly enough to sell the house anyway!). There is a lot of ego and self-esteem tied up in home ownership. Moreover, to friends and family the idea of selling the house to get your capital into aggressive (and risky) investments will often seem preposterous. They will wonder what is wrong with you; wonder if perhaps you are going broke (or mad!)

Not many people end up selling their homes to get their capital working better for them. They look for their starting capital (or for more capital) elsewhere, and often decide that they do not mind waiting longer for financial freedom. We understand such emotional attachments and do not usually push too hard. However, it is very important that you understand the financial implications of having almost all of your capital tied up in a home and that you're aware of the full range of options.

Not owning a house and renting for a few years is certainly a way to free up capital and make a good start on the road to financial freedom. The numbers do not lie. This illustration uses very simple figures.

Let's say you own a house worth $200 000, which is mortgaged to $100 000. You could either sell it and invest the $100 000, or carry on living in it. Let's see how it looks in seven years' time.

Option 1: Carry on living in it. At 5 per cent growth (a little higher than the rate of inflation) the house will be worth $281 420. You will have paid $56 000 of interest plus around $20 000 for rates, insurance and maintenance.

Option 2: Rent and invest at 15 per cent. You pay approximately $12 000 a year in rent, and the $100 000 that you have invested will be worth $266 001.

	Option 1 Stay in house	**Option 2 Rent and invest**
Capital profit	$81 420	$166 001
Less costs:		
Mortgage interest	($56 000)	
Rates/insurance/maintenance	($20 000)	
Rent		($84 000)
Net position in 7 years	+ $5420	+$82 001

Option 2, renting, makes you $82 000 better off. That is a fairly steep price to pay for home ownership, a feeling of permanence and security!

Even when they see these numbers, most people still choose to stay in the house. If you do that, you must see your house as a Security Asset. It is unlikely ever to have the growth that will make you rich, so cannot be seen as a Wealth-creating Asset. As a Security Asset, your house is actually quite good. House prices are not particularly volatile and therefore it provides a good store of wealth. Further, the mortgage payments that you make will usually (although not always; see below) be in part principal repayment. This means that you are increasing the equity and therefore the amount that you have in Security Assets. A further advantage is that a mortgage 'forces' you to save. Being better off renting assumes that you invest the money you would otherwise have put into home ownership—and many people do not have the discipline to do that.

Having said that, we encourage some people to stop paying off the principal of their mortgage, suggesting they pay interest only. These are people who have quite a lot of equity in their houses, but very little (or nothing) in Wealth-creating Assets. Going onto an interest only loan will mean that your monthly mortgage payments are smaller and you can use the difference to invest aggressively.

We encourage some others to increase their mortgage repayments. These are people who already have quite a high proportion of their net worth in Wealth-creating Assets and need to more rapidly shift wealth to their Security Assets.

This is all a part of the balancing which is such an important part of gaining financial freedom. It has to be done on an individual basis and the mix depends primarily on a client's starting position and how fast they want to travel.

Home ownership is a great Security Asset and is right for most people. However, it is worth doing the numbers to see what the house is really costing you and how much it is holding you back from the drive to your dream.

Chapter 25 | Some people already have enough

When we see a new wealth-coaching client, we always do a net worth statement first. Occasionally we find someone at the extreme end of the spectrum, who is already in fact quite wealthy, who either does not believe that they are wealthy or cannot break the habits of a lifetime. There are people, especially those who have a farm, a business or are in property, who already have a high enough net worth to be financially free (if they ever stopped for long enough to do one). These people have all their wealth, often quite considerable, in their farm, their business or property activities, and have nothing much in anything else. They are certainly wealthy, but they do not have financial freedom.

People with a business may have spent years running and developing it. They have continued to plough everything they make back into it. It uses all the available cash flow, and takes all their time, leaving nothing for an improved lifestyle, or anything for other investments. These people are on a treadmill, running ever faster to grow the business without really knowing why they are doing it. They may be wealthy, but they are often not very happy. They do not have the lives they want in spite of their wealth. They have a lot in valuable assets but lack the most valuable asset of all—time.

Businesses have a voracious appetite for both capital and time. These businesses may be very profitable, but the owners use up all those profits to fund growth. Profits are there, but cash flow is nevertheless tight. Without a plan to take money out and put it into other areas, they use all the profits to go on and on doing the same thing—building the business.

Property people can be the same. They spend years buying properties and developing a portfolio of good investment properties. As they get growth in their properties, they use that growth to gear up and buy more property. Their gearing level remains high, and over the years they seldom allow themselves spare cash for anything. The habits of years stay with them—they keep on gearing up to buy more property.

Worse, perhaps, this group is resistant to investing outside the property area. The idea of developing a Security portfolio never occurs to them, or if it does is rejected out of hand (they do not want to use capital for Security because that would take away their ability to buy properties and add to the portfolio). So everything that they have is in that continuously expanding group of properties.

Both these groups, property people and business owners, feel poor, and that they are running ever harder to stay in the same place. In fact, they are not poor and not staying in the same place—they just feel they are. While they are getting richer, they are asset rich but cash poor (and even time poorer!). They are not getting any closer to financial freedom because their wealth is not in the right place. They are rich, but they are not free.

On paper, both groups are wealthy. Theoretically, both could sell up and retire to the Gold Coast. They do not do it because in part they do not really deep down believe that it is possible (even though the numbers say that it is) and because they have no idea what they would do with themselves.

Their real problem is that they lacked a vision to explain why they were doing this right from the start. They have never had a dream of financial freedom that was specific enough or compelling enough to make them stop. The wealth-creating activity has become an end in itself because they have never really known what the endgame was!

To be fair, these people often say that they love their businesses and their properties—they love the games that they are in. They do not want to retire to the Gold Coast (or anywhere else). If that is what they want in life, who are we to argue?

However although we do not argue too much, we know that they are neither happy nor content. They have a feeling of dis-ease: doesn't life have more than this? How come I have to keep running faster and faster when all I really want is to go fishing? They may say they are happy running their businesses, but they often are not.

Furthermore, they are continually playing double or quits. Even if they do not want to sell up and get out of the game, at the very least they should be shifting some of their income (and probably some of their capital as well) into Security Assets.

Claude's case illustrated this well. We met Claude about fifteen years ago. He was 67 years old, full of energy and drive. He had run a moderately successful importing business for the last 30 years and was about ready to retire. He owned the business and a house, but not much else. His plan had always been to build up the business, sell it on retirement and live on the proceeds.

He approached us because the plan had just come unstuck. The business was ready to go on the market but he had just lost the New South Wales agency for the goods that he imported. He had represented the overseas company for the last 30 years, but the company had just been sold and the new owners had decided to use their Victorian agents to cover New South Wales. Claude's business was wrecked, and within weeks it was in receivership.

Businesses fail all the time, as do property investments, sometimes through little fault of the owners. We cannot say it often enough: if you play double or quits with your Wealth-creating Assets, one day the dice will be against you and the result will be quits.

If you are already quite wealthy, take another look at your net worth and see how much you have in Security Assets. If it isn't much, plan to shift some of your wealth across to them. If you are already quite wealthy and want financial freedom, you will have to move quite a lot of your wealth into Security Assets. You do not have to stop being in business, you do not have to stop farming, nor do you have to stop managing your property portfolio—but you do need to limit your wealth-creating activities or at least have them grow more slowly.

Once again, you need to get a clear idea of why you are doing what you are doing, develop a dream for the future and plan to get to it. Financial freedom could be a lot closer than you think, if that is what you really want.

Chapter 26 | Some people already earn enough

Income by itself is not much use. Either you need to have the right sort of income (passive income) or you need to use the income that you have very well to build up wealth and financial freedom. When you have enough passive income from your investments, you have financial freedom. When all your income comes through work you don't have financial freedom; you have to do some things to build Wealth-creating Assets. This has to be done by saving, and saving aggressively.

Wealth and riches are about capital, not income. This is especially so for that group of people who have high incomes from their jobs. They have to divert a large proportion of their income into investment areas—save it—and turn it into capital that will grow and ultimately give them passive income. This group is not building a business which they will be able to sell so they need to build something else; perhaps a property portfolio which they run along with their jobs or some kind of quite aggressive set of investments.

People who have over $100 000 a year in salary are doing very well by most standards. But many of them are not making much progress towards financial freedom. They are not building anything other than their careers.

They are not progressing towards financial freedom for one of two reasons:

- **They consume too much** Consumption tends to go up as income rises—a better house, a better car, overseas holidays—and then they buy a boat! These people often have the appearance of wealth (they have all the toys) but all they really have is income—which they spend. That is not wealth—it is merely income that stops when they stop working.

- **They allocate their income poorly** Even when there is something left over from their conspicuous consumption, too much of it goes into Security Assets, not enough into Wealth-creating Assets. People on very high salaries can often afford to take some risk to build their wealth more quickly. Rather than solely making contributions to the super scheme, they need to get out and have their money work harder. Right now they are making their time and skills work for them; they need to make their money work for them too.

A lot of income may pass through your hands over the course of your career, but if you do not build a good asset base, you will never have financial freedom. Only that asset base can give you the passive income that you will need for financial freedom. If you are in this position, you have to get some Wealth-creating Assets; look for higher yield investments and get your money working.

You may be able to earn your way to financial freedom through a career. But if you want to do it in any reasonable sort of timeframe, you will have to reduce your consumption and allocate more of your income to something that will work hard for you.

Kate and Stephen were professionals in their early forties—she was an accountant, he a lawyer. Their combined incomes after tax were around $140 000. Kate approached us because she felt that something was wrong with the way that they were managing their money: in spite of all of their income she felt that they were running ever faster, working ever harder and were really not making themselves any better off.

We did a net worth statement:

Assets		
	House	$650 000

	Cars	$200 000
	Shares	$5000
		$850 000
Liabilities		Nil

Stephen and Kate had put all their money into lifestyle type assets (cars and the house). They had used their high incomes to pay off the mortgage, but since the last payment had been made, they had not developed any further wealth.

Kate and Stephen had two main problems:

- Aside from the private school fees for their children they had no idea where their money was going. We got them to develop a budget and at the same time carry a notebook to record all their expenses. Over a period of about three months we all got a clear picture of where the money was going (holidays, restaurants, treats, and so on) and managed to get an expenditure plan that gave them a $4000 per month ($50 000 p.a.) surplus without significantly altering their lifestyles or denying them the really pleasurable things. If ever there had been a case of money being frittered away mindlessly, this was it.
- They had none of their capital in Wealth-creating Assets—it was virtually all in Security Assets (the house) or being consumed (the cars). They were not developing anything that could one day be sold. They had, however, developed their careers and although these could not be sold, the income from them could be used. We decided to invest all the surplus from their budget ($50 000) into growth shares which Stephen could manage.

Kate and Stephen's dream was, by the time they were 50, to work only six months each year and spend the other six months doing aid work in developing countries. We showed them that if they invested their annual surplus of $50 000 and successfully got 15 per cent, in ten years they would have $1 100 000.

Stephen and Kate's plan looked like this:

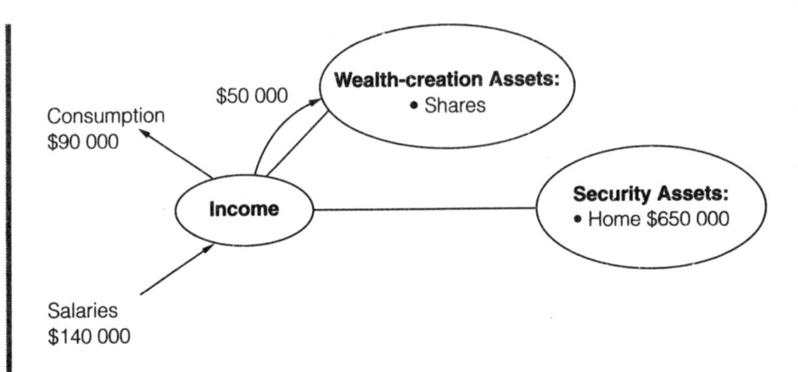

In ten years' time, Kate and Stephen would have the house worth $650 000, and shares worth $1 100 000. In ten years' time the shares could be cashed up and the proceeds moved to Security Assets that would give them an income of at least $50 000 per year after tax—not enough for freedom, perhaps, but a very good supplement to the other work they would continue to do.

Part V

Getting rich

Chapter 27 | Wealth-creating Assets

Let us now start thinking about the things that are going to make you wealthy and how you can use them. For most of those who have not thought much about money and wealth, it is often the Wealth-creating Assets that seem to be the hardest part to get their heads around. For most people, the really big question is: How do I get rich?

In fact getting rich is not really the hard part at all, provided that you:

- have the desire to be rich;
- are prepared to take some risks;
- have a strategy to manage those risks; and
- are patient.

You *can* accumulate the sort of wealth that you need. As we have already shown you (and we will discuss this further) there are ways of getting 15 per cent and more on your money. They are not without risk—but they are out there.

Chapter 28 | What Wealth-creating Assets are out there?

The things that are going to make you wealthy, that will grow your money at a fast enough rate, must meet two major criteria:

- They must produce a 15 per cent return of income and capital, after tax and any fees. You must be growing your *wealth* at this rate.
- They must be saleable; that is, the Wealth-creating Asset must be able to be sold by you in the fullness of time, and owned by someone else. You cannot become wealthy by growing an asset's value if you cannot sell it at some point in the future. This precludes using your career as a Wealth-creating Asset. Yes, there are a few people who become wealthy through their careers, but not many. To get wealthy through your career you must, first, have a very successful career, and second, make sure that you do not increase your consumption each time you get a pay rise.

Given these two criteria, we know of only three things that you can own to make you wealthy:

- a business;
- property investment and development; and
- shares.

Each of these is discussed in more detail later. Your job at the moment is to choose which one is the vehicle to make you rich.

People often don't really choose what will make them rich; rather, they go into some sort of activity almost by default. Thus, they go into a particular business because the opportunity arises, into property investment because they attend a seminar, get into shares because of a tip from their cousin, etc. There is no great thought given to the matter, no detailed consideration from which a reasoned judgement could be made.

This is not necessarily a bad thing. You must have some sort of affinity with what you are going to do for the next ten or even twenty years. You are hardly likely to keep up enthusiasm for that period of time unless it is something that you want to do.

Some people try to choose their wealth-creating activity, the sort of business or property to go into, by analysing and then entering the business (or property type). Although this kind of analysis is reasonably straightforward when applied to buying shares, it is often difficult to do properly when setting up or buying into smaller businesses. Making your choice of Wealth-creating Assets using this process seems fairly obvious, but in reality, without some affinity with the activity, or a point of introduction to the industry, it will be hard.

Therefore most people will choose how they are going to become wealthy by looking at activities that they are already involved in, already have some interest in or already have some knowledge of. This choice by default may not sound like the best way of going about things, but it does at least mean that you go into something with a bit of a head start.

Nevertheless, before you start, before you commit any capital, double-check that the activity really is capable of making you rich. It does not have to be the most likely way to riches but it does need to give you a fairly good chance. Two important points here: do not enter into an activity or industry you know nothing about solely because it seems to be in the most rapidly growing sector; and, do not go into any activity or industry, no matter how passionate you are about it, which is in rapid decline.

Chapter 29 | Choose only one

Your Wealth-creating Assets are the opposite of your Security Assets. Your Security Assets are spread around—a diversified portfolio of quality investments that require little or no looking after. Wealth-creating Assets still require quality, but not a spread of a whole lot of different things. Getting rich requires concentrating your assets, staying rich requires spreading them. Your Wealth-creating Assets need to be focused on just one area—a business, some properties or shares—but *not* all three areas.

Some people try a lot of different things to make them wealthy, one of which they hope will come off. They might own some investment properties and dabble a bit in shares and then set up a business and after a while push that business into areas outside its core concerns.

That's the wrong approach. We know very few people who have become wealthy by chancing with a whole bunch of things. You are far better off concentrating on just one thing—and doing that thing well. Certainly this is risky, but that risk is reduced by the focus and care that you bring to the activity. You can have all your eggs in one basket, provided that you make sure that it is a good basket, you keep the basket in good repair and carry it over the ground with a firm footing.

People who become wealthy do it by having one really good activity that they put all their time and energy into. They live, eat and breathe this activity—it occupies them completely.

That sort of commitment is what you need to get rich. You have to know everything there is to know about your activity—all the gossip about who is doing what, where the markets are heading, where the gaps in the market are, where the biggest opportunities lie. You do not get that sort of intelligence by spreading yourself across several different, unconnected things. You get it by concentrating and focusing on one specialist area.

Remember that you are (in the early days at least) putting nearly all of your capital into this one thing. Drive it hard, and guard it carefully.

Chapter 30 | Don't fish in a dry ditch

To grow your wealth, you have to choose for your Wealth-creating Asset an industry or an activity about which you are passionate. Be wary here, however, for you can quite easily be passionate about things that are likely to lead you nowhere.

You may already have a business or be in some kind of property development or other activity, and not be making any headway. You may have spent years struggling along, and found that no matter what you do, you cannot make money.

It may be that you are fishing in a dry ditch—that is, there are simply no fish there to catch. In that case, do what any half-reasonable angler would do—pack up and move someplace that does have fish. There is no point throwing good money and good time after bad—you need to get your capital and your energy working.

The other thing to look at here, even if you are making profits, is whether you are building up something that one day will be saleable. Are you developing goodwill that can be sold? The answer in many cases will be 'no'. There are some business types for which no buyer will pay a premium for ownership—in those businesses very little goodwill can be developed. This is particularly so in service industries where there is easy entry for other players. You may, for example, build up a car repair workshop. This may be reasonably profitable, and you may have a good client list. However, when you come to sell, will someone pay handsomely for that client list? Car repair is an industry that is easy to get into; any journeyman mechanic can set up a workshop and start to gather customers, and is unlikely to want to buy an existing customer base. This is the case for a lot of the trades and professions—the ease of entry is such that new players see no need to pay a lot of goodwill.

To sell something with a lot of goodwill, there needs to be some certainty that the business is sustainable, and that the customers will not leave with the old owner. Service industries, trades and professions are usually business types where loyalty does not attach to the brand of the company, but rather to the individuals within the company. That means that the goodwill goes out the door with the individual practitioner.

Worse, there are some industries and business types where you will never make money, most often because the markets for the goods or services concerned are poor with very low margins. There are no fish in this ditch at all. If you are doing something that is not building value, get out of it. Be ruthless and spend no more time fishing that dry ditch.

Therefore, while it is important that you choose for your Wealth-creating Asset something that you know and are passionate about, it is pointless to choose something, no matter how much you love it, that is never going to make good profits and at the end of the day will not be saleable. Will there be someone willing to buy what you have developed, or can they just as easily set up their own operation? Will the technical skills necessary (as in motor mechanics) put people off buying into your business? Are there barriers to entry? Are there good enough markets and good enough margins that someone will want to buy your business?

If you are considering what will make you rich and have an option or two, ask yourself these kinds of questions as a check. Certainly you need to have an affinity with what you are going to do, but if that activity cannot be developed into something profitable that will make you rich, keep looking.

Chapter 31 The anatomy of scams

Most of us, at some time or another, are offered opportunities that promise overnight riches. Some of us are offered these things on a regular basis: hardly a week goes by without a call from a broker in Manila offering shares in Celestial Heavens Electronics Corporation Plc at 14 cents or the opportunity to earn 50 per cent a month through Prime Bank Debenture Rollovers. Even those Nigerian email offers are still around, and still getting people to provide their bank account details. Some usually very astute businesspeople are had occasionally, and those who are less astute are had on a much more regular basis.

One of the big things that trips up people who are trying to become rich is that they try to do so too quickly. They are so set on becoming rich that they fall for just about any get-rich-quick scheme on offer. You have to be careful in your drive to become rich, because you may be very tempted to take shortcuts.

To get rich and stay rich, you have to avoid these kinds of things. Getting rich is nearly always a long and sometimes winding road—and there are not many shortcuts. There are a lot of scams around—and if it sounds too good to be true, it probably is.

Scams have their own anatomy. They nearly always have three easily recognisable features:

- They offer very high returns.
- You have to invest *now*—the promoter does not want to give you time to think, and so creates some urgency for you to invest.
- The minimum amount that you can invest keeps being reduced. The promoter tells you first that the minimum

investment is $100 000. When you do not say 'yes' to that immediately, you will be told that you can buy half a unit at $50 000, and when you are still reluctant you are told that they can bend the rules a bit and let you in for just $10 000.

We have had a lot of phone calls with these features (you probably have too). The callers can be very persistent, and employ sophisticated sales techniques. However, these schemes are not the way to get rich (and certainly not the way to stay rich, except perhaps for the promoters). Concentrate on your core wealth-creating activities and leave the fringe get-rich-quick schemes to others.

Chapter 32 | Successful wealth creators manage their business

People committed to creating wealth must make their Wealth-creating Assets perform really well in order to give returns on investment in excess of 15 per cent a year.

You may already own a business or be considering buying or setting one up. You may be involved in property investment or intend to enter that field. Some of you may have a share-trading portfolio or intend to divert income into aggressively managed shares in the future. Whichever of these you are involved in, you will have to manage your enterprise well to achieve the high returns you are seeking to make you rich. Whatever you are doing, think of it as a business, and copy what the best owners and managers do. You must apply best practice to whatever you do, be it shares, business or property investment.

What do the smart business owners and managers do? Well, there are libraries full of management books, case studies and research material outlining the best practices of successful businesses. You can learn from this material, doing what the best and smartest do. There are several key ideas that you will find helpful.

Keep your eye on the future

Smart business operators are always scanning their surroundings, looking at what is happening and where the trends which will affect their business are heading. If you are already in business you need to keep an up-to-date grasp of the market; if you are about to enter a business you want to think about where the gaps in your market will be. For example, if you are involved in the food industry in any way, things that you might take into consideration include current concerns about food safety (for example, GM and GE foods, hygiene), the declining size of households, more working women, lots of singles, ready-to-eat food, emphasis on freshness and health, concern about diabetes/fat, etc. Any or all of these factors may impact on the business you are in or will be in. Property investors look for big market shifts, such as an increasing demand in certain areas for property that can be used as educational establishments or student accommodation. Smart businesspeople work *on* their business, not just *in* it. You cannot afford to keep your head stuck inside your business and ignore what is going on around you. Not only do you need to keep an eye on the future, but you must also be able to continually adjust your plans for the business in line with what you see. Create a picture or dream of what your business could become and start to move it in that direction.

Look for opportunities and threats

Smart businesspeople have a keen sense of where the openings will be in their market and position their business to take advantage of them. Following the example above, a smart business operator in the food industry might look for an endorsement of their product from the Diabetes Foundation, might explore providing healthier (but yummy) food to schools and institutions that have a responsibility of care, might target single, diet-conscious, young women with lots of disposable income, might take a lead in labelling food regarding traceability, etc. Similarly, smart businesspeople ask where their business might be threatened. Will you risk being pushed out of business because your standards are low, because your packaging is no longer good enough, because you are at risk of a product recall, because someone else could better supply the supermarkets you have been selling to? Good businesses have a risk management plan that identifies the things that might go wrong so that they can be actively managed and reported on.

Be clear-headed about strengths and weaknesses

Smart businesspeople are very honest with themselves about what they are good at and what they are not. They never attempt to fool themselves. They know where they stand relative to others in the field. They take steps to stay ahead in the areas where they have strengths and they take steps to remedy the areas where they are weak. If you are known for your modern, attractive, easy-to-use packaging you would want to ensure that you continue to lead the field in this area. If your systems are poor, resulting in incorrect or incomplete deliveries, you need to set remedying this as a priority. Strengths and weaknesses really only matter in connection with your opportunities—you don't have to be fantastic at everything but you do need to excel in the areas where you have the opportunity to excel. Similarly, you cannot afford to be weak in areas that are threats to the survival of your business—for example, hygiene in the food industry.

Know how your business works

This sounds obvious, but many businesspeople do not fully understand their business model. In other words, they don't know how their business fits together, don't really understand where money is made and lost, don't fully appreciate what really matters and what does not. It's essential that the key people in your business all work to the same understanding. A good test is to get every member of staff to try to draw a diagram of the business. That often shows that you do not share the same 'picture'—

small wonder that we get such confused and wasted effort in so many businesses! Sometimes this sort of analysis shows that your model has shortcomings that sheer effort alone will not overcome; in other words, your model may be fundamentally unprofitable! (In this case you will need to get some help to re-engineer your set-up.) Smart businesspeople know what the key 'drivers' of their business are—what are the few critical things that have to be managed really well in order to succeed. As in every other aspect of success, it is critical in business to be able to separate the vital few areas from the many that are relatively unimportant. For example, top property investors know that it is the market for *tenants* that is most important, and so they study it and know it well. They are clear that what is vital to their business is the ability to attract tenants who will pay an ever-increasing top dollar. When you are clear about what areas are vital you can work on those areas to ensure excellence, and to streamline those processes which are central to your business.

Know how you intend to 'win'

Every business needs to have some competitive advantage. Will you win through service? Speed? Price? Quality? Brand? Convenience? Location? Being first? If you are just the same as everyone else in the industry, then how will you make very good profits? What is it in your industry that you could do better than the others that will matter enough to the customer that you either get more business or can charge a premium? Can you go the extra mile for the tenants of your property investments so that you are known as a good landlord? Such advantages are hard to sustain, because the ones being left behind will usually try to catch up quickly. Good businesspeople are always looking for the next area where they can create an advantage, however short its duration.

Measure what's important

You can't manage what you can't measure. And you can't measure everything. In line with the above, identify the areas that are critical to your business, and what you need to know in order to measure success and progress in these areas. Then develop good indicators. Property investors will measure their vacancy rates carefully. If you are in the food business, your distribution might be critical to your success. Good delivery records will be essential to keep your contracts with a supermarket chain. A key indicator of your performance will be 'in-full, on-time' delivery. You might set an acceptable level of 99 per cent for this indicator and measure the success of the people involved against that. It means you know how you are doing, it means you have information to share with your key customer (the supermarket) and it means your whole team is focused on achieving these standards rather than the on hundreds of other things they might be diverted by. You cannot manage or improve your business without information.

•

In our experience, good businesspeople are always working on their total business rather than getting immersed in the daily and urgent detail. They can see the wood from the trees. They usually have an acute sense of what drives their business, they know how value is created in the business and what are the key areas that need careful management. They use this knowledge and insight to align the efforts of everyone in the business, putting the best people where they are most needed, putting resources into the areas most critical to success. They always know how the business is performing against key measures—and they use this information to better manage the business.

Chapter 33 | Successful wealth creators manage their people

Winning in business is increasingly about winning the so-called 'war for talent'. In other words, your business is dependent on you having a good share of the best people. There is a worldwide shortage of people with the skills that business needs. You have to compete in a 'market' for people and the success of your business depends on your ability to attract and retain great people around you. Make no mistake—there is a global marketplace for good people. Every developed country in the world is seeking people with skills and the rest of the 'right stuff'. The Western democracies in the Northern Hemisphere are acting like giant vacuum cleaners, extracting the best from elsewhere in the world by offering great conditions of work and superior opportunities. The people that you will want to work with you have lots of choices—why will they choose you and your business over others?

Smart businesspeople know that they must be attractive to great staff; otherwise they will have to try to run a successful business with mediocre or poor staff. That is not a winning proposition! If your staff are not as good as the people working with your competitors, here or overseas, what are the implications? Note that this can be just as important for property or share investors—they need the top industry people (real estate agents, brokers, bankers, etc.) to work with them just as much as any business needs good staff.

So what do the smarter businesspeople do? There are several areas on which they focus, in which they invest resources, and measure performance:

Recruitment

The key issue here is to ask: How will you attract people to work with you? You don't necessarily have to be employing them; you may just want to 'recruit' someone as a partner, an ally, or even a key member of your wider network (more about networks later). Your reputation is your main weapon for attracting others. Winners work with winners. What do others say about you? What do people say about your business or business skills? What are you like to work with? Are you a good employer? What would current or previous employees say? What would colleagues say? Your reputation as an individual and as a business owner is very important to your success in the future. Do an audit on where you stand, get some feedback and do what you need to do to build a great reputation. And remember that you are always in recruitment mode—even when you haven't got a vacancy.

Total reward package

The key question that the people you are trying to attract around you in any role will be asking is: 'What's in it for me?' You need to be clear about what you are offering, and your offer needs to be competitive. Sure, pay matters but the better people are looking for far more than competitive pay. Are you good to be around? Do you care about other people? Is the culture in your enterprise positive and supportive? Will people want to be led by you (are you taking them anywhere)? Will you inspire them? Can they be their best around you (or do you make everyone ordinary)? What does the future look like with you? Are you going places? Are they going to be part of something that they can be proud of? Will there be other good people in your enterprise?

Development and opportunity

Remember that good people have choices. Good people can always command a fair wage but what the better people want is the opportunity to grow and develop, and to be worth a lot more in the future and have even more choices! They will be asking about your plans for their training and growth. They will want to know how being around you will lead to their development. They do not wish to simply get older working with you; they want to get better! If you are not going to be trying to do anything worthwhile or challenging, or if you have no interest in taking them along, then why would they waste their time/lives working on your business?

Retention

If you have been good enough to get some great people to work around you keep asking yourself why they should stay. We have seen many businesses destroyed by the exit of a key person who was taken for granted (in both small and large organisations!). Key people are invaluable. Your business is the people who work on it, in it and around it. You should take care of these people like the treasures they are. One great person is worth several lesser people, and the smaller your enterprise the more important this usually is. Never take good people for granted—they have choices! Would *you* stay?

Network

It would be easy to think that the only people you needed to worry about were employees. Not so. More than ever before, it is essential for businesspeople to manage a greater network well. Corporations generally have specialists to help with relationships with key stakeholders, but all businesses, even one-person businesses, have key stakeholders. You will need to consider how you develop and maintain good relationships with suppliers, clients, customers, professionals, contractors, community, interest groups, etc. It is harder today than ever before to do everything yourself—the success of your endeavour will depend on lots of other people and the quality of their relationship with you. The web of *who* you know is essential to your success. If you have poor interpersonal skills, or are low in what is currently called emotional intelligence, you need to put some effort into developing these skills. Happily, they are learnable! This is an area where a coach might be of great help.

Board of directors

There is a reason why large companies have a board of directors—the members of the board can provide independent advice and oversight about the direction and governance of the business. While there is no requirement on a small enterprise to follow suit, it is a good idea to pick the best features of this system and use them to your advantage. Many smaller businesses would benefit from having one or two independent directors. They can provide a 'sounding board' for the owner and help with the consideration of key decisions, having the advantage of not being tied up in the everyday 'busyness' of whatever is going on. For the small amount of expense and time involved, the payoff is huge if you choose your directors well, people who should bring key skills and experiences that complement those of the owners. We have seen several small enterprises take off with the input of a couple of external directors/advisers. Even if you do not wish to constitute a formal board, you can apply this thinking to an informal 'sounding board' of friends, advisers, coaches and contacts from other industries.

Experts

One of the pitfalls for the entrepreneur is to believe that you can do everything yourself! Smart businesspeople make very good use of experts—accountants, lawyers, patent attorneys, real estate agents, property managers, sharebrokers, consultants, tax attorneys, investment specialists, trust lawyers, among others. Figure out the critical needs of your Wealth-creating Asset and get a 'heavy' in the field to assist you. You need great people on your side—and your heavy needs to be at least as good as the one you are facing! It is often hard to locate great professionals. Ask around, get references, and when you find good ones treat them well and make sure you have a great working relationship for life.

•

Remember, your enterprise will never outperform the people in it. It's all about the team you build. Who do you dream about having on *your* team, playing on *your* side? Do what you need to do to get 'em and keep 'em!

Chapter 34 | Successful wealth creators manage themselves

You are committed to becoming rich or you would not be reading this. To create wealth you are going to have to manage some wealth-creating enterprise very well. You will also have to manage a wide team of people so that enterprise can thrive. But the most important thing for you to manage is *you!*

Your Wealth-creating Asset won't outperform you. How good do you need to be to manage your Wealth-creating Asset so that it returns in excess of 15 per cent a year? Or, put another way, how will you keep up? You are the most important asset in your enterprise—and you need to keep developing and improving. What will you need to do to get a good return on yourself? Are *you* getting better by 15 per cent each year? Why not? What would you need to do to improve yourself by 15 per cent each year? The smart people we come across who create wealth never, ever, stop trying to improve themselves.

So what do they do? Well, the really smart ones understand that the skills and levels of thinking they have today won't be good enough for tomorrow. They focus on four areas.

Knowledge

What do I know? What do I need to know? Smart people are aware that the knowledge they have today about their area of business won't be enough for the future. So they work to find out what they need to know . . . they read books and trade journals, attend seminars, listen to tapes, search the Net, and so on. Successful people ensure that they have deep knowledge of the area in which they intend to create wealth. You do not need to be an 'expert' but you have to know enough to succeed in the future in your area. Get the knowledge you need to create wealth. Keep your knowledge increasing along with your wealth.

Skills

What can I do? What do I need to be able to do? Smart people are continually auditing their skill-set and making sure that it is up to the task at hand. This could range from realising that it's time to be able to create a spreadsheet on the computer to figuring out that learning to play golf could enhance your network considerably! A key question to ask is: 'What is the key skill that is holding me back?' In other words, 'What is the skill that, if I mastered it, would transform my ability to create wealth and achieve my dreams?' Get the skills you need to create wealth.

Attitude

What program does your 'headset' play? What program does your headset *need* to play? The wrong attitude holds people back more than anything else. Examine your attitudes to success, to wealth, to achievement, to your own abilities. Are you programming yourself for failure every day by rehearsing negative ideas, or are you playing on your own team by encouraging yourself every step of the way? Surround yourself with positive people, people who achieve, and those who will support you to succeed. Avoid 'toxic' people—the ones who don't believe in you and who don't believe in themselves, those who probably have never made and will never make the effort to achieve anything. Unfortunately, many people tell us that they have such people in positions very close to them! Our advice in those cases is to guard your dreams well (that is, don't tell anyone who is likely to be a 'knocker' of your plans), to work even harder to maintain a winning attitude, to go and find other people to support you. Get the attitude you need to create wealth.

Habits

What do you actually do? What do you need to do? You may have the knowledge, skills and attitude that you need for success but unless you actually do what is necessary daily, weekly, monthly, you will not succeed. What bad habits do you have? What good habits do you need to replace them with? Are you poor at returning phone calls? Do you neglect to take care of yourself and then find you become sick and cannot take care of your Wealth-creating Assets? Do you lack the discipline to work at the relationships that are essential to your success? Do you need to develop the good habits of planning and aligning all your activities with your dreams and goals?

•

The smart people who create wealth work hard in the above areas. They do not force themselves to be good at everything—rather, they are very focused on the knowledge and skills they need to master, on what attitudes and habits they need to be able to claim as their own. They understand that life gets better when they do—and they do what it takes!

Chapter 35 | How wealth works: The engine of compounding

Albert Einstein said that compound interest was the eighth natural wonder of the world! It is, especially if you are serious about becoming rich. But the good thing about compounding is that you do not have to have Einstein's brains to understand it and make it work for you. Compounding is really just some very basic arithmetic.

So, how does it work? When you have money to invest you earn interest on the use of that money. For example, when you lend your money to the bank, the bank pays you for the opportunity to use your money. This is described as the interest rate and is expressed as a percentage for every year the money is loaned, for example, 5% p.a. In the same way, if you are late in paying your credit card bill, the bank charges you for the use of that money until you pay it. Credit card interest rates are often over 20% p.a. (note the difference in rates!) But the principle is exactly the same. So, if you lend someone $100 at an interest rate of 10% p.a. you are owed $110 a year later. You get your capital (or principal) of $100 back and you also get an interest payment of $10. Simple interest, simple sums.

Where interest becomes almost magical is where it is reinvested and allowed to compound—that is, when profits are retained and reinvested. Following the example above, you could lend your $100 again, *and in addition lend the $10 of interest you had earned.* Now you are lending $110. At 10% p.a. this will earn you $11 of interest. In the next year you have $121 to lend that will earn $12.10 in interest . . . and so on. The 'original' $100 is continually reinvested and the interest earned is also reinvested. Each year your capital stake grows and each year even more interest is earned. You are now 'earning interest on the interest'. This is why we talk of the 'rich becoming richer'. (It works in reverse as well. If you get into debt that you cannot pay, the money that you owe also compounds so that the poor can easily become poorer.)

Unfortunately, many people have had bad experiences learning maths at school. Often the only thing standing between you and more wealth is the (lack of) understanding of some simple arithmetic. If you hate maths, stick with this chapter—we guarantee that it's the most useful maths lesson you will ever learn! And it's painless—you will learn to love your calculator!

Let's look at that $100 again.

You have $100 to 'invest' and can get a rate of 10% p.a. If you invest your $100 you will get $10 in interest. You can spend the interest ($10) and invest the $100 the following year and get another $10 dollars, which you can take, spend, whatever. This is called 'simple interest' as it is obviously simple—you continue to have the same amount of capital ($100), you continue to invest it at whatever rate you can get (10 per cent here) and you earn a sum of interest ($10 here) which you take and do with whatever you wish. At the end of ten years you have your capital—$100—and you have also earned ten lots of $10—another $100. You have $200 in total.

It looks like this:

Year	Capital	Interest rate	Interest earned	Interest spent	Total at year end
1	$100	10%	$10	$10	$100
2	$100	10%	$10	$10	$100
3	$100	10%	$10	$10	$100
4	$100	10%	$10	$10	$100
5	$100	10%	$10	$10	$100
6	$100	10%	$10	$10	$100
7	$100	10%	$10	$10	$100
8	$100	10%	$10	$10	$100
9	$100	10%	$10	$10	$100
10	$100	10%	$10	$10	$100

Now, let's look at the difference if you compound the interest; that is, you add the interest earned each year back into the capital sum and reinvest the new amount:

Year	Capital	Interest rate	Interest earned	Interest reinvested	Total at year end
1	$100	10%	$10	$10	$110
2	$110	10%	$11	$11	$121
3	$121	10%	$12.10	$12.10	$133.10
4	$133.10	10%	$13.31	$13.31	$146.41
5	$146.41	10%	$14.64	$14.64	$161.05
6	$161.05	10%	$16.10	$16.10	$177.15
7	$177.15	10%	$17.72	$17.72	$194.87
8	$194.87	10%	$19.48	$19.48	$214.35
9	$214.35	10%	$21.44	$21.44	$235.79
10	$235.79	10%	$23.58	$23.58	$259.37

What is the difference between simple and compound interest? What is it that means one investor has $259.37 while the other only has the original $100? The answer is that one has taken out the interest each year and spent it. The other has left the interest in the system and let it compound so that each year there is interest earned on the interest. If you think this is an insignificant amount try the example with an investment of thousands. You can do this yourself on a very ordinary calculator. You will probably find the numbers so exciting that you will rush out to buy a financial calculator—a great investment.

The really critical things to consider as you play with these examples are:

- the amount of capital;
- the interest rate; and
- the number of investment periods (years).

Obviously the amount you invest makes a very real difference. However, even if you are only at the beginning of your path to wealth and have very little to invest, do begin. Compounding works so well that there is no cause to delay.

Secondly, the rate of interest makes a huge difference. Try the above examples using 9%, 8.5%, etc. and note the impact of even a 0.5% or 1% difference.

Thirdly, time is your most important ally. This is why so many investors are more focused on time in the market than on timing the market. It is only as time goes on that you really see the huge gains of compounding; the early years don't look that spectacular but as time goes on the effect is huge. Compounding begins slowly but the effect gets greater and greater. Most people don't wait long enough to see the benefits; it is common for people to make investments, tire of the unspectacular returns in a few years, and withdraw their money before they have received the benefit of time. Younger people often don't have much capital but time is truly on your side and you should use this advantage. Having said that, it is never too late! If we graph the effect it looks like this:

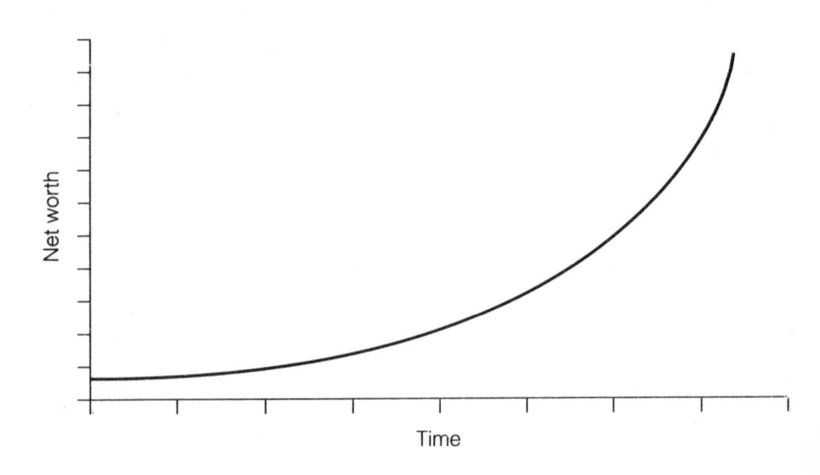

The above examples are very simple and straightforward; you can easily see how they would apply to bank deposits. However, the compounding principle works just as well for a Wealth-creating Asset, whether it be a business, property or shares. In fact it works a good deal better, because the returns from your Wealth-creating Assets ought to be at least 15 per cent (much higher than the example of bank interest given above). A return of 15 per cent that is reinvested in your business, properties or shares will see your wealth grow very quickly. The rule of 72 (see page 43) tells you that at a 15 per cent return your money will double every 4.8 years.

Whether you invest in a business, in an investment property or in shares, you will almost certainly derive income from the investment, paid in the form of dividends/profits, rentals or share dividends respectively. Smart investors will reinvest at least some of this income in their preferred investment vehicles: business owners will retain earnings; property investors will reinvest in the property or another one; and share investors will buy more of the same or other shares. Not only is the value of their original investment rising (if they have made a good initial investment) but also their reinvestment adds to the compounding effect. When you plough income back into the assets, income from these assets grows even more. This in turn leads to the asset value being re-rated upwards (assets are ultimately valued by the income they produce). You would also expect a smart investor to have some expertise in their chosen area of investment and be reinvesting in a business, property markets or share markets that they know quite a lot about and that should be expected to perform. This is the 'virtuous circle' of wealth (see page 20). Clearly the effects far surpass bank deposits if you get it right, as the rate of return (above 15 per cent) is much better than bank deposit rates (about 5 per cent).

If you can grow the capital in your Wealth-creating Assets at 15% p.a., your wealth will double every 4.8 years. This means that if you start with a business worth $100 000 and you get growth of 15% p.a. (reinvested profits plus increase in asset values), it will be worth $200 000 after 4.8 years, $400 000 after 9.6 years, $800 000 after 14.4 years . . .

•

Compounding, the idea of reinvesting your profits, is the engine that will make you wealthy. And it's an engine that will happily take a turbocharger . . .

Chapter 36 | How wealth works: Turbocharge by leverage

For an even better result, you can add to the effects of compounding by borrowing money to add to your initial capital. How does this work? Let's look at the example of a property investor (it is easy to borrow money for property investment). Suppose you saw a rental property that you would like to invest in that cost $100 000 but you had only $20 000 available. You could borrow $80 000. Your $20 000 is the owner's equity, the amount of the money in the property that is actually yours. Let's say that you have to pay 10 per cent interest on the loan—that will be $8000 a year. For the sake of simplicity, let's assume that the rent you get for the property is also $8000. So your rent covers the 'cost' of the loan each year. (You will pay this every month/year and not let the debt compound!) You will pay only the interest and not any of the principal amount ($80 000) that you borrowed. Imagine that in five years' time the property is worth $150 000. You sell. You pay back the loan and are left with $70 000. Your owner's equity of $20 000 has grown to $70 000. The value of the building has compounded and you have been able to avail yourself of this effect but without using much of your own money. While the property rose 50 per cent in value (from $100 000 to $150 000), your capital has risen 350 per cent (from $20 000 to $70 000).

You have used someone else's money to cash in on the effect of compounding. You have in effect 'turbocharged' your investment of $20 000 and received the benefit of the compounding on a far larger sum. The return on your $20 000 over five years has been nearly 29% p.a. (that is, 29 per cent compounded each year), just about double our benchmark of 15 per cent. Borrowing to buy good income-earning assets, whether a business, property or shares, is how smart people get wealthy.

Borrowing to invest in this way is variously called 'gearing' or 'leveraging'. It's easy to see why these debts are so called—you get the effect of using a bigger gear or of operating a giant lever. (Archimedes said he could move the whole world if he had a lever long enough!) You are using other people's money to add to your initial stake and getting the benefit of the compounding of the total sum. Essentially, leverage is about making other people's money work for you. But you only have to pay back what you borrowed, not the money you made with that money!

Businesses almost always borrow money to achieve this effect. If they are good at what they do, (that is, profitable), then it is logical that they should do more of it and return the benefit of the extra money generated to the shareholders. This gives shareholders a much higher return on the equity they have in the business than if there were no borrowings.

We are often asked how highly geared or leveraged a business should be, but there is no right answer as it varies from business to business. In general, the principle is that if you can make more money with the borrowings than it costs to have the loan, it is worth having some borrowings. Obviously you have to assess the costs of the borrowing and the risks that you are taking. Many highly profitable and growing businesses pay out no dividends because they are making the judgment that it is more in the shareholders' interest (that is, they will get a higher return) to have this money reinvested in the business. Conversely, when a business is holding a great deal of cash/paying out very high dividends, you should be asking why they cannot find a better use for the money. (Clearly, it is a little more complicated than this and is greatly influenced by factors such as the particular industry, the business cycle, the product life cycle, and so on.)

Property is similar. It is often easier to borrow to buy property, as there is a real asset for the bank to reclaim should you default on your loan. You can invest in property in this way with very little of your own money—10 per cent or even less. A good investment property will give rentals to cover some or all of the interest repayments and the loan can be repaid when you sell. If you buy well to begin with you should achieve a very handsome return through the leverage of your borrowings. Many property investors will own several properties that are financed and geared in this way.

Similarly for shares. In fact, if you look at Chapter 50, you will see that it is just as easy to use other people's money to buy shares as it is to borrow to buy property or take out an overdraft for a business.

Gearing really works for Wealth-creating Assets because of the high returns. Borrowing to buy things which return 15 per cent or more makes great sense when you are only paying 8 per cent for the money you have borrowed.

Now to state the obvious: this all works in reverse as well! Leveraging or gearing is a wonderful way to turbocharge compounding which works to make you rich. Equally well, the turbocharge effect can make you very poor, even bankrupt. The acceleration works in both directions—if your business wobbles, if your property purchase drops in value, if your shares go through the floor, you not only lose your own money but the borrowed money as well. Although your Wealth-creating Asset is worth less, the borrowings are still the same size—and ultimately the 'other person' will want his/her money back. The debt will rapidly compound when you are unable to pay even the interest, never mind the principal. This is the process by which many seemingly very successful people go spectacularly broke. (See Chapter 6, The 'vicious spiral' of bankruptcy.)

The key thing to remember is that while leveraging makes a good investment better it makes a bad investment even worse!

Chapter 37 | How wealth works: The return on *your* money

Putting up a little of your own money and using a lot of someone else's to buy a high-performance asset is how people become rich. It does not really matter what the high-performance asset is, provided that you can borrow against it, and that it provides high returns. Smart people know that they need to use other people's money to lever the relatively small amount of money that they have at the start. They know that the game is to increase their wealth—to keep driving up their net worth until they have enough for financial freedom. They want their Wealth-creating Assets to grow and grow, and for their share of those assets to be greater and greater.

Clever people know that they need to keep getting a high return on their money, so that their equity continues to grow. This return on your money is called the 'internal rate of return'. This is jargon for the rate at which you are growing your own money, the rate at which you are growing the equity that you have in your property, share portfolio or business. This, of course, is the only thing that is important: the rate that *your* capital is growing will dictate how much you have in the future.

The internal rate of return is different from the return that the Wealth-creating Asset is getting. For example, an investor buys a property at $110 000 with a $10 000 deposit and borrowings at $100 000 at 8 per cent interest. The rent is $10 000 p.a. after all costs.

This investor has made a profit of $5000 on the $10 000 that was invested. This is an internal rate of return of 50 per cent (the investor has 50 per cent more equity than at the start of the year). While the property is not a particularly high-performing one (only 3 per cent capital growth), the investor has quite

Property value	$110 000
Borrowings	$100 000
Equity	$10 000
Rent	$10 000
Interest	$8 000
Cash profit	**$2000**
Capital growth (@3%)	*$3000*
Total profit	**$5000**

successfully used gearing to rapidly grow the quite small amount of initial equity.

This example is illustrative only; it is to show how good investors get high rates of return and grow their net worth quickly. The example is in some respects unrealistic because, for example, it doesn't include any provision for tax. This next example, however, is both realistic and true.

> The couple started farming at age 26. They had married a few years before and with her job (teaching), his fencing contracts and buying, doing up and selling a few houses, they had managed to save $47 000 at age 26.
>
> That $47 000, with some borrowings, was enough to start them off as share-milkers. As they grew their wealth they added to their herd until they could buy their own farm, borrowing to buy out neighbours 'when they were feeling a bit depressed'.
>
> Today, fourteen years on, they have a farm which, with stock, plant and buildings is worth over $3 million. Their borrowings are at $500 000 They therefore have a net worth of $2.5 million. This couple has grown their net worth from $47 000 to $2.5 million in fourteen years. That is a rate of return on the $47 000 they started with of 33 per cent (that is, an average 33 per cent return, compounded every year, for fourteen years).
>
> They have worked very hard to get where they are—long days and few holidays. They have taken high risks: they have nearly gone broke

> three times, twice when the price of milk fell badly, and once when the weather meant a very poor season. They report having had some major 'slanging' matches with their bankers!
>
> This is one very smart couple—they are good farmers, good with the finances and good businesspeople. At age 40, they could easily sell the farm and sit back and enjoy the freedom that they have created. Interestingly, they have no thought of 'retirement'—they love the lifestyle of the farm. They are making some changes though: we are working with them to develop a Security Assets portfolio (some secure off-farm investments) and to take on some more staff so that they can get a bit more time for holidays and so that they can work *on* the business rather than *in* the business.

The key thing for you to think of is how fast you can grow the capital that you have now. Use the engine of compounding by retaining most of your profits, and turbocharge the engine with leverage. It is the turbo that will give you the grunt that you really need. The use of other people's money is the way to grow yours.

Chapter 38 | Using other people's money

Successful entrepreneurs borrow as much money as they can; they are seldom short of an idea for making money, and the only thing stopping them is a lack of capital. Having a level of debt is almost inevitable as you grow your wealth. The amount and structuring of your debt has a very large effect on your security, however. Successful entrepreneurs, those who have been around the game for a while, know that bad things do happen. They also know that poorly structured borrowings can lever those bad things so that they become disasters. Those who are determined not just to get rich, but to stay rich as well, structure their affairs so that they will survive if something really bad happens. That is why we suggest that you have some of your wealth in Security Assets, safe investments that are tucked away, quarantined from the other things you are doing. It is also why you should structure your borrowings as safely as you can.

The key to safe borrowing is to give your bank as little security over your assets as possible, and as few guarantees as possible. This is often much easier to write than to do—security and guarantees are requirements of most bank loans; banks will not advance any money without them.

Banks like to take a belt and braces approach—that is, they want all the security over all the assets that are available. They also want any guarantees available, whether those guarantees are personal from you and a member of your family, from another one of your companies or from your Family Trust. Banks like guarantees because they allow the banks ultimately to get at all the assets that are owned by your family. If you personally guarantee your borrowings, the bank can call on you if something goes wrong and may eventually force the sale of all your assets.

The only things that might be safe are those that are in a trust, and only then if the trust has been formed early on and has not agreed to guarantee your borrowings.

While banks want all the security and all the guarantees that are available, you want them to have as little as possible. This is for two reasons:

- If something does go wrong, you do not want other people, other entities and other assets caught in the problem. You want to be able to isolate or quarantine off certain things that you own. There is no point in having assets in the Security compartment if your lenders can go straight to them for any unpaid money.
- You want flexibility so that you can borrow more money in the future. If you have already given the bank security over everything you own, you cannot easily go back to the bank and ask for more borrowings. However, if you have managed to keep out, say, one of your rental properties or a seaside apartment, you are able to go to a different lender and borrow against it. This might be very useful if you spot another opportunity that looks very profitable, or you have some financial difficulties and the ability to borrow a bit of extra money to tide you over will make all the difference.

This is then the borrowing game: the bank wants everything it can get as security; you want to give as little as you can.

It needs to be said that in the early days at least you are unlikely to be able to borrow without giving a good amount of security (perhaps you *will* have to give security over everything that you own). You will also not be able to borrow without giving a personal guarantee, perhaps a personal guarantee from your partner/spouse, and a guarantee from other companies and trusts controlled by your family. It is unlikely at the beginning that you will be able to borrow much without giving in to these bank requirements.

However, as time goes on you should aim to keep certain items unencumbered (particularly things that are in the Security compartment). You should also aim, over the years, to get rid of as many guarantees that you can. The goal is to get rid of the mortgages, debentures and guarantees that you have to give the bank to be able to borrow. That is necessarily a long-term goal, not something that will happen overnight, but is certainly a goal worth working towards. Those who have financial freedom usually have little or no borrowings, and they certainly have no guarantees from other family members or other entities.

Chapter 39 | Reducing securities and guarantees

The guarantees that you have to give lenders often tie your assets together in a way that poses high risk. For example, you may have paid off the mortgage and own your home outright, but if you have given it as security to the bank for a business loan, it is vulnerable to any failure in that business. Similarly, personal guarantees demanded by the bank may mean that anything else you own can be pursued in the event of the failure of your business. We often come across clients who have a large portfolio of assets, some of them debt free, but which are *all* vulnerable owing to the guarantees that exist between them. The whole edifice could come tumbling down very quickly in the event of failure in one part. People often feel that their assets are a great deal safer than they actually are, when in fact one unforeseen event could topple them all. Your guarantee means that you must cover all of the obligations of the debtor, 'joint and several' if there are other guarantors.

When you have a loan (or want to get a loan) from the bank a kind of game is played: what the bank wants and feels it needs in order to lend the money, versus what you wish to avoid when borrowing. The 'game' looks like this:

The bank wants:
- your personal guarantee
- as much security as possible
- your partner's guarantee
- company/trust guarantees

You want:
- to give no guarantee
- to give as little security as possible

There are ways of reducing the amount of security and the number and extent of guarantees that you give your lender. The following eight key strategies are invaluable in playing the 'game'.

When the bank asks for your personal guarantee

When you give this, it means that you personally guarantee all of the obligations of your company (which may own your business, property developments and investments). If your company goes into receivership or liquidation and there is a shortfall to the bank, it can come to you for that shortfall, pursuing you to bankruptcy if necessary. At the beginning there will be no way to avoid giving a personal guarantee; the bank will not lend the money without it. However, as time goes on and your company and business get bigger, and your borrowings are reduced, you may be able to negotiate away the guarantee. The way to do this is to get the bank to agree to release your personal guarantee when your company's indebtedness is reduced to a particular level. For example, if your company is borrowing $500 000, to be repaid over fifteen years, you might be able to get the bank to agree to release your guarantee when the loan has been reduced to $200 000.

When the bank wants your partner's personal guarantee

This is something to resist as much as you possibly can. If your partner also guarantees the company's borrowings, anything that he or she owns will also be vulnerable if trouble strikes. The best way to manage this is to be sure that your partner is not a director of your company. Then you can say to the bank: 'My partner has no role in the business, he/she has taken legal advice and no guarantee is available.' The ball will now be in the bank's court—to decide whether to make the loan or not. If the bank decides to decline the loan on the basis that it wants your partner's guarantee, you can always have your partner change his or her mind and make the guarantee available. However, it is well worth trying to withhold your partner's guarantee in the first instance.

When the bank will want a debenture over the assets of your company

Give it to them; it is in your interest. A debenture is a form of security over the assets of a company. It is a floating charge, meaning that it secures the stock (and other assets of the company) as they are owned at any point in time. A debenture gives its holder (usually a bank or other lender) priority in getting money from the sale of the company's assets in the event of insolvency. It also allows the holder to appoint a receiver, someone who is charged with managing and selling the company's assets so that the debenture holder gets its money back.

The reason you want the bank to have a debenture is that the bank most likely also has your personal guarantee. If the bank does not have a debenture it will get paid in the same proportion as all the other creditors if your company gets into financial trouble and is liquidated, and if there is a shortfall in what the bank is owed it can come to you under the personal guarantee.

If it has a debenture, it will get paid in priority to the other creditors, making it much more likely that it will get paid in full out of the company's assets, and therefore will not need to use the personal guarantee to make up a shortfall.

When the bank wants collateral security

Collateral security is held on other things you own rather than on the thing that you are borrowing to buy. For example, if you are borrowing $100 000 to buy a new pie-making machine, the bank will take that machine as security, and will also want a floating debenture over your company's assets. It may also want a second mortgage over the house. The first two of these are reasonable—you are likely to have to agree to the security over the new machine and the debenture over the company's assets. However, you should resist the second mortgage over the house, because this may well stop you borrowing in the future, and if things do get tough, the bank can exert a great deal of pressure on you. As in the case of your parnter's personal guarantee, the way around this may be to negotiate the release of the second mortgage security when the loan is reduced to a certain level.

When putting initial capital into your company

The initial capital that you put into your company should go in as a loan from you to the company, rather than as share capital. Similarly, any future money you put into the company should also go in as a loan. We often find that when people start a company to own a business, their lawyer and/or accountant (the people who are helping them start the company) advise them to put the money in as share capital rather than as a loan. If you are starting a company and are putting up initial capital of, say, $25 000, this money is better put in as $500 for the shares of the company, and as a loan of $24 500. The point of making a loan instead of putting your money in as share capital is that in the event of liquidation or receivership, loan monies are paid out in priority to share capital. You could even secure the money you have advanced by way of a second debenture (a bank is likely to have a first debenture), which would mean that you would get paid in priority to unsecured creditors.

When you repay a loan

When you have repaid a loan, make sure that the security is released. Quite often, when a loan is repaid the bank will suggest that you leave the mortgage or debenture in place. Their rationale is that you are likely to have to borrow again, and it will save you money in legal fees if the security has not been released. The thinking is correct in that it will save you money; however, mortgages or debentures left in place have sometimes been forgotten for years. At some point there is some fresh borrowing with the bank (or perhaps the giving of a guarantee for one of your children) and only when things turn bad on that loan is the extra security that has been in place for years remembered. Having kept the security in place, the bank is in a far better position than it would be otherwise. There have been quite a lot of cases where this sort of thing has happened. It may cost you a bit of extra money to have the security released and have it put back for new borrowings, but that is money well spent.

Avoid guarantees from the entity that owns your Security Assets

The whole point of Security Assets (such as your family home and your diversified portfolio of low-risk investments) is that they are *secure*. The purpose of having them in a separate entity (like another company or family trust) is to quarantine them from the risk that is inherent in your Wealth-creating Assets. You lose all this security as soon as you give a guarantee from this entity to cover a debt. If you must, and this can often be the case early in your wealth-creation process because you have nothing else to offer as security, then make sure that it is the first security to be released as you repay the debt.

Try to lower bank/finance company debt

Smart businesspeople use their trade suppliers as much as they can to fund their business, and at the same time make sure they collect their debts quickly and efficiently so that they are not funding someone else's business. Taking as much credit as you can from suppliers, and doing your debt collection well, means that you have less need for working capital. This means that your overdraft and/or other bank debt will be lower. In effect, you can swap your secured bank debt with credit from your trade suppliers (that is also unsecured).

•

Intelligent entrepreneurs who are in the know work hard to keep their risks low. This is the 'survive to thrive' syndrome. A big part of this is structuring borrowings well and negotiating with your lenders to keep securities and guarantees to the minimum.

Part VI

Creating wealth: Business, property, shares

Chapter 40 | Wealth-creating Assets: Your business

It is probably fair to say that more people become wealthy through ownership of a business than in any other way. This was not always the case; there was a time when property investment was the easiest way to riches. However, with low inflation and high real interest rates (the rate of interest after inflation and tax have been taken into account), property investment has become a much more difficult game.

However, although some people become wealthy through a business, a lot do not. A high percentage of people fail, with their business folding in the first few years. This is not necessarily because the business idea was not good. Nor is it necessarily because of poor management or under-capitalisation.

The real problem, in our experience, is attitudinal.

Contrary to general opinion, most people who start businesses are not entrepreneurs—they are technicians. They come to business ownership with the attitude of the technician rather than the attitude of someone who is in business.

Ask almost anyone who owns a small plumbing business, for example, what he does for a living. He will not say, 'I am a businessman'; he will say, 'I am a plumber'. Ask a partner in a law firm what she does and she will say she is a lawyer. The same goes for computer consultants, financial planners, hairdressers, landscape gardeners and so on. All these people come into their businesses with the attitude of a technician first, and a business owner second. Their profession or trade takes most of their focus, not the business.

These people work *in* their businesses, not *on* their businesses. Management tasks (finance, marketing, human resources, customer relations) are interruptions to their day. Their attitude is to get on with fixing people's pipes or transferring their properties rather than developing a valuable business. In fact, their businesses are little more than slightly glorified jobs. The main task of each day is to perform their trade or profession rather than run the business. In effect, these people are self-employed rather than running a business.

For a business to be both successful and valuable, it has to be able to run without you the owner. It cannot be simply an extension of you and what you do (your trade or profession); it must be a stand-alone enterprise that can be sold.

This is important if you are going to build something that is valuable, if your business is going to make you rich. No one will buy it, or at least buy it at a good price, if it has nothing more to it than you. People who are buying a business know that they cannot buy you with their purchase. They know that they can restrain your trade (stop you trading for a period in a defined area), but when you sell the business to them, you leave and they are on their own. They therefore want something that is not dependent on you, but can be run by anyone.

Building a business that is like this is what most people overlook. Most business owners are so concerned with increasing profits that they do not build something that can last beyond them. In fact, to get rich, profits are less important than the capital value of the business. Profits and income are certainly important (they lead through to the value of the business and are the way that goodwill is valued), but those profits have to be sustainable, and able to be passed on to a new owner without interruption.

Remember that financial freedom is a capital game—to be rich you have to build something that is of high capital value. Yes, the income from it is very important. However, the real objective is to build something that will greatly increase your net worth. You want as much income and profits as you can—but this is mostly so that the business has a high value when it is time for it to be sold.

When you are planning your business, you should be thinking about who is going to buy it and what might stop them going ahead with a purchase. Even though you may have no intention of selling for a decade or more, there is no point building something that will not have value to other people. It is just as easy to build something that is saleable (and therefore valuable) as to build a business that can only ever be an extension of your job.

People who are buying businesses are looking for good sustainable profits. It is those profits that mean that someone will pay goodwill, which in turn will make you rich. People will not buy a business if they believe that on its transfer to their ownership the profits will leave with you.

Chapter 41 | The glory that is goodwill

The development of the goodwill of a business is the fastest and surest way to becoming rich. Goodwill is wonderful because it is basically wealth that comes out of thin air. Goodwill is not a tangible 'real' asset that has to be purchased from retained profits. It is something that can be developed in the normal course of business without any additional investment being required. Goodwill is a reflection of the fact that you have chosen a good business to get into (one with high barriers to entry) and run it well. Most service businesses (plumbers, builders, consultants, etc.) have very little goodwill because such businesses can be started up easily.

Goodwill may be an intangible asset, but it is real enough when it is converted to cash on the sale of the business. Some businesses sell with very large amounts of goodwill.

If you have run your business well and profitably and it is difficult for others to come in and compete, someone who wants to be in your kind of business will prefer to buy your business and pay high goodwill rather than start up from scratch.

Goodwill is a premium; it is the extra money you are paid when you sell your business, above and beyond what the tangible assets are worth.

When someone buys a business, they buy two things:

- **Tangible assets** These are things like plant, equipment, machinery, motor vehicles, stock, etc. They are the hard, real assets that are necessary for the running of the business. They have been purchased with the owner's cash either at the start of the business or out of profits during the life of the business.

- **Intangible assets** These are things like goodwill, brands, licences and concessions and restraint of trade (the person selling the business promising not to go back into that type of business for a number of years). The intangible assets have been developed seemingly out of thin air, but have a value because of, and based on, the ongoing profitability of the business.

People going into a business have the choice of buying the tangible assets they need and going into business from scratch as a start-up, or buying an existing business that is already up and running.

Goodwill is the premium that the buyer pays to get a ready-made business. Its amount is calculated largely by the profitability of the business. As a general principle, a business will be worth somewhere between three and eight times its annual profit after the owner's salary. (There are lots of exceptions to this, but this basic idea applies to the sale of most businesses.)

Therefore, if a business is making $100 000 p.a. net profit after tax and after a salary for the owner, and a multiple of four is used, its total value would be $400 000. In simplistic terms, this is how businesses are valued: people pay an amount for the business to get them a return on their capital that they think is justified given all the circumstances of the nature of the business. If a business was making $100 000 p.a. profit, a buyer might agree to pay $400 000 for it because they would be getting a return of 25 per cent on the $400 000 that was invested.

The new buyer in paying this amount gets the total business: all the tangible assets, and all the intangible ones as well. In a way, the amount of goodwill is simply the residual amount between the price of the tangible assets, and the total price for the business. As such, it can be regarded as the balancing amount—it balances the amount of the plant, equipment, stock, etc. with the amount that the total business is worth and being sold for.

For example, a business being sold for $400 000 may have tangible assets of $150 000, so the purchase price is made up of:

Tangible assets		
	Plant	$40 000
	Motor vehicle	$50 000
	Stock	$60 000
Total tangible assets		**$150 000**
Goodwill		$250 000
Price of business		**$400 000**

Buyers now have a choice. They can buy the business that is for sale at $400 000, or they can set up from scratch. If they want to set up from scratch, they will have to go out into the markets and buy the tangible assets that the business requires. For $150 000 they could buy plant, motor vehicles and some stock. They could then set up the business and develop it, all for $150 000. The trouble with this, of course, is that it is likely to take some time (possibly even years) for the new business to reach a good level of profitability. The people who set it up will need to find staff and suppliers, establish systems and processes, and develop the market and customer base. In doing this, there is a good chance that they will make mistakes, and spend a lot of time with little or no profit. In addition, there is an existing business in the market (the one that was for sale but which they did not buy) with which they are going to have to compete.

If the buyer resists the temptation to start up from scratch, and buys the existing business for $400 000, certainly that means that they have paid $250 000 more for ownership (that is the amount of the goodwill), but they have also bought some considerable advantages:

- The systems are all developed.
- The markets and customers know that the business exists and are used to buying from it.
- Suppliers will continue to supply their goods and services.
- Staff are in place and trained.
- The sellers of the business will not compete against the new buyers.

All these things (and more) add up to one very important point: from the day the new owners pay their $400 000 and take over the business, it will be profitable. Right from the first day, there will be income. The new owners will not have to spend time in developing business systems, training staff, finding customers, and so on. The business simply continues under the new owners as it had under the old ones.

That is why people pay goodwill—for the continuation of the business and its profitability, so that the stream of earnings and profitability is uninterrupted.

When you are setting up a business think of what you are building from a buyer's point of view. Will that buyer want to buy your business as a whole or set up from scratch (and therefore compete against you)? People will pay handsomely to avoid the hassles, the risks and the financial implications of starting from scratch. You need to make sure that your business is of a type and so well run that anyone wanting to enter your field has no choice but to buy it and pay goodwill.

Chapter 42 | What makes a business valuable?

Goodwill is your reward for running the right business in the right way, the premium that a buyer will pay over and above the value of the assets because the business uses those assets efficiently and well to make good profits.

To make a business worth a lot of money (and therefore to make you worth a lot of money) you need to work at developing goodwill. A high goodwill value is how people become rich through their businesses. However, only some businesses attract a high goodwill figure; in certain industries businesses will only ever sell for a little goodwill, and these are, of course, industries to avoid if possible. Many forms of consultancy are like this, as most of the goodwill from customers accrues personally to the consultant rather than to the business. Even though the consultancy may be quite profitable, it will not be able to be sold with a lot of goodwill as it walks out the door with the consultant.

Businesses that are valuable:

- **Have good sustainable profits** No-one will pay a lot for a business if they think the profits that have been made are not going to be ongoing. A buyer will want to be confident that the profits and therefore the return on investment are going to continue.
- **Have growing profits** Most buyers will want to be able to improve and enhance the business to make better profits. A smart business buyer knows that if the profits can be increased the value of the business will increase in proportion. The example in the previous chapter showed a business with profits of $100 000 a year being worth $400 000. If the profits can be increased to $150 000, then, all else being

equal, it will continue to be worth four times its annual profits, and so be worth $600 000.

- **Are not dependent on any one person** The business should be independent of you not only in a process or technical sense (others should easily be able to do the work or sell the product), but also in a marketing sense. It is not a good idea to have your name attached to the business (John Smith Printing Ltd). This makes it harder to pass on the goodwill to someone else; it is far better to have a generic name, like Ace Printing Ltd.
- **Have good systems and processes** The business can be easily managed and run without your minute-by-minute intervention (McDonald's has such good systems that the business can be run by teenagers).
- **Are not easy to copy** Perhaps this is because of location, strong branding, a special recipe, distribution network, exclusive stock or agencies or some other special factor. Some sort of barrier to entry stops (or at least slows) others from setting up a similar business.
- **Have a likely end-buyer** It is good to know what sort of person (or company) is likely to be the eventual buyer of your business. You may think that your engineering business would be ideal for a farmer who is retiring to town, your chain of four shops valuable to a large retailer who is in competition with you, or your fruit juice company valuable to a large corporate already in the food business. It does happen that people develop good businesses that do not have a natural buyer. This can be especially so when the value gets too high for most individuals to contemplate (over $2 million is too high for even most retiring farmers) but is not high enough for a corporate to think worthwhile (as it is less than $5 million).

You need to find a business that you can get passionate about, something which is a good fit with who you are. However, run checks on your choice: will it be something that can be built up and sold? Will people want to buy it and pay for the privilege? Can you build a business that is so good in your market that no-one will want to take you on from scratch? These are really important questions, ones that need thinking through before you start to create an even bigger enterprise.

Chapter 43 | Think like an owner

You need to own a business, one with value that can be sold, not some glorified form of self-employment. This means that you have to think like an owner, working *on* your business, not *in* it. That means trying not to get too bogged down in the detail of what happens every day but keeping removed somewhat so that you continue to think strategically.

More than this, thinking like an owner means directing and managing your business in a way that enhances its value long term. You own a valuable asset and your plan must be to retain and develop that value. This means always doing things that are good for the reputation of the business, continually developing the brand so that it is something very desirable. It means taking a long-term view, not cutting corners and taking some small short-term advantage. There is a bigger play involved than making a quick buck—that means working on the quality of your product or service, developing staff and going the extra mile for customers. All these things cost, but the pay-off comes with a better business, one that is worth more.

If you think like an owner you will do things that will increase value. There are lots of things that are important but we will talk here about the three main ones.

Building a great team

While everyone says that their staff are their greatest asset, most people are only paying lip service to the notion; their actions do not bear out their words. Most business owners look after their other assets well—they maintain their vehicles, keep their stock safe and oil the machines in the factories. But they do little or nothing to maintain their staff. They have good programs for plant and machinery maintenance but nothing for people maintenance. The machines get their regular service; the staff get no extra training.

You should hire the best people, train them and then do what you have to to retain them. Yes, this is expensive—but people build businesses. Training and development is an area that most small and medium sized business owners largely ignore, at great cost to their businesses. This lack of training is largely about cost. But, although it is expensive to train people well and then have them leave, it is even more expensive to not train them and have them stay!

The aim is to have a business that does not need you. You can't do that if you have staff needing constant attention in order to get anything done. Send them to courses, train them and develop them. Your role is to set strategies and coach your people to get the best out of them.

Networking

In many ways, all businesses are networks. The best of them have the best networks—of customers, of suppliers, of staff and of professional advisers. Your business needs to be at the hub of a very big network, and you need to use that network to your advantage.

Nowhere is this more important than for industry information. You need to know what is going on. You need good open lines of communication with your customers, your staff, your advisers and within your industry. You will not always know what is going on but someone somewhere will. Your network should be able to give you the connections you need to know what is going on in any part of your business and your industry.

That means getting out and talking with (and listening to) your staff every day. It means joining trade associations and other businesses and going to their functions. It means attending seminars and meetings, taking people for breakfast or a coffee. The relationships that you have with people are critical for the success of your business.

Planning, planning, planning

As the owner of your business, you are the leader. To lead effectively you have to know where you are going (it is fairly hard to lead a group somewhere if you do not know where 'somewhere' is).

As an owner, your role is about strategising and setting plans. The strategy is to build a valuable business, the plans are how you are going to do that. Plan the work and then work the plan.

Only good planning will keep you focused on your final goal. Only good planning will ensure that you make the right decisions to add value. No planning means that you will make ad hoc decisions, reacting only to the problem of the moment. Good planning means that decisions are made and there are systems in place to deal with problems.

•

Stop being a plumber, consultant, hairdresser or whatever. Get yourself a new career as a business owner and welcome the planning, strategising and management as the core of your job, not as an interruption to fixing pipes or cutting hair. Think again about your dream for financial freedom: that will be fulfilled by owning a valuable business that is well managed and will be easily sold for a premium price.

Chapter 44 | Property riches

Many people in the past have become rich by investing in property. Many also use it as a store of wealth, as part of their Security Assets. Property investment can be all things to all people—it depends on how you go about it. There is more about how property can fit into your Security Assets in Section VIII. This section is about using property to become wealthy.

Many people almost instinctively think of property investment when they are planning how they are going to become rich because there are many famous examples around the world of people becoming extremely wealthy through property.

However, although it is still possible to become rich by investing in property, it is no longer as easy as it once was. Property investment used to be the lazy way to riches. With high inflation and low real interest rates, you could buy just about anything and do well. The only impediment to becoming wealthy through property investment lay in the amount of money that you could borrow.

The game was to borrow as much as possible and buy as much as possible—and wait. Within a few years, inflation meant that the property had risen in value, allowing you to borrow more money to buy yet more property. A decade or two of this saw a substantial property portfolio—and great riches. To be successful required little analysis, a simple strategy and no particular expertise or knowledge of the markets. It required neither hard work, nor homework, and was a game that could be played (and won) by just about anyone.

Times have changed, but because the stories are still around of lots of money easily made, it is little wonder that people still think property when seeking to become rich. But remember it is not as easy as it was—it is no longer the lazy way to riches. Now. you do need to analyse and be well informed—you have to go into property in a professional manner, for it will not automatically make you rich. You have to put in the work to get a better than average return, one sufficient to make you rich quickly. There are still plenty of people becoming rich through property investment, but there are even more who are trying and failing.

Property is attractive as an investment in part because there are so many examples of people who have done well from it, in part because of the many books and seminars on the topic, and in part because of its heavy promotion by real estate agents. However, many promotional schemes are simplistic, glossing over the difficulties that property investors face. Property, like any other Wealth-creating Asset, requires hard work and homework to be a winner.

Property, for a lot of people, is an attractive way to get rich for a number of good reasons.

- **Property is easy to borrow against** You can buy property, and become rich on other people's money (a bank's). This allows you to make a start with very little of your own money, and if you get things right you can keep on borrowing against the increase in value.
- **Property gives two returns** Those are income from rents, and capital growth. While the capital growth side of this is unlikely to be as high as it once was, it is still likely to be considerable for those who buy well. Along with the capital growth, there is likely to be growth in the income from the property, which over time greatly improves the total returns.
- **It is tax efficient** Property investors in most countries are treated very well in terms of tax, being able to claim interest depreciation and other costs. Capital gains are not taxed in

some countries, while in other countries CGT regimes are benign.
- **Property is not a particularly volatile investment** Its value tends not to fluctuate widely. As such it is relatively safe (but not, of course, completely without risk).
- **Property investors play with big numbers** A relatively small percentage increase in value can be a significant increase in the investor's net worth.
- **There are bargains in the property markets** Property markets are not perfectly efficient, and there are often properties that can be bought well below their true value.
- **Properties can be enhanced** You can do up properties to increase their value well beyond what you spend on them.
- **Property investment is the dealmaker's dream** Those with good negotiating skills can use them to their advantage when dealing with vendors, purchasers, tenants and financiers.

Property has a lot going for it! At low gearing rates (with little borrowings), an average property will be quite a reasonable investment for your Security Assets. It will give moderate returns with low risk.

However, if you want to get rich from property you will have to adopt a different strategy. There is a lot that you will have to do, but the two big factors are:

- buying well; and
- managing actively.

These are the topics of the next two chapters.

Chapter 45 | Buy your property well

To get rich through property you have to buy the right things. You have to buy properties that are significantly undervalued or properties that will grow in value at a rate higher than the average. Preferably you will do both.

Properties that will grow in value at a higher than average rate are usually well located. Location or position is the most important factor in high capital growth rates. There are certain regions that over time give far more growth than others, giving investors not only high capital growth but also high income growth (the rents rise along with value of the property). This has always been the case and will always be the case.

Good locations are those where people want to live and, in the case of commercial and industrial property, where businesses want to have their premises. It is really about as simple as that: where there is demand from tenants, rents will rise and capital values will go up too. This is especially so where there is some natural feature (a harbour, river or hill) or council zoning regulation which limits the supply of property. If no more can be built, demand from tenants and owners will outstrip supply and rents and values will rise.

You do not necessarily have to spot these locations early on—a good high-growth location will tend to remain that way (provided demand does not dry up for some unforseen reason). A location which is close to the CBD or with a view of the harbour is likely to continue to show high growth over years, decades, and probably centuries.

The problem with properties in such locations is that they are hard to buy (and even harder to buy as a bargain). Yields (the amount of rent you will get compared to the value) tend to be very low, which means they are hard to finance. You will have to outlay a bit more—for both the price you have to pay and the amount of deposit you have to find.

This may mean that you own less property than if you buy in poorer locations. However, you will get better growth. You can use that growth over time to buy more property, using the additional equity and income that the growth has provided to purchase more property. This may mean refinancing, but if you want to get rich through property you will continue to gear up to buy more when you can.

The second strategy is to find undervalued properties. Spotting and buying bargains is both great sport and a great way to drive up your net worth. There are always bargains available in property markets. This is especially so when times are bad—when the economy is bad you should be very active. When the markets are booming, as they do periodically, you should sit back and enjoy the growth you are getting from the properties that you already own and wait for times to get tough again. The real winners in property are those who are able to buy when all the commentators and experts are saying how terrible things are. In good times keep your powder dry (and your money in the bank) so you can fire your shots when all the other players are lying down nearly dead.

We have wealth-coaching clients who will only buy if they can do so at 10 per cent below true value. Others look for 20 per cent discounts. Yet others look for properties where they can add value—by spending, say, $20 000 to put on an extra bedroom where they know this will increase the value by $50 000. These property investors look at a lot of properties and put in a lot of offers. That most of the offers are rejected does not bother them; they will only buy if a property meets their criteria.

Some of our clients are really property traders; having purchased a property they put it straight back on the market (perhaps after titivating it a bit with a coat of paint). These clients often do not care about location; as long as they are confident that they can flick the property on quickly and at a profit, they are happy. Others always buy in reasonably good locations because they want to hold on long term.

You can find bargains—there are lots out there if you really go and look hard—but you probably won't find them in top locations. Taking your time and putting in the effort, however, buying 10–20 per cent below market value, is a very good way to get rich.

The things you have to do to buy your property well are:

- **Study the market you are interested in** You have to become an expert in your particular location, knowing every property that is for sale and the prices they have sold for. Perhaps even more importantly, you need to know about tenant demand and the rate of vacancy in your area. You need to know better than anyone the value of what you are looking at.
- **Be patient and persistent** You may have to look at a lot of properties before you find the right one. Don't be disheartened when the right thing does not come along quickly. You may also have a lot of competition from other buyers. It's worth sticking with it until you beat them all to a choice plum.
- **Develop your network** Get to know all the good real estate agents. Top properties are often never advertised—good agents make a phone call to the right person and it's gone. Make sure that you are that right person. Get to know good financiers, mortgage brokers, valuers, property managers, other investors, etc. Go to seminars and meetings of property investors so that you know everything that is going on.
- **Remember that the costs of buying and selling property are high** You must build this factor into your plans. The key is to buy right. If you buy right you will not want to sell. If you do decide to sell there must be plenty of fat in the system to cover your costs.

Chapter 46 | Manage your properties actively

When you go into business as a wealth-creating activity you know that buying the business or setting one up is only part of what you need to do. Certainly you need to do that well—but managing the business well is just as big a part (in fact it is probably more important). It is the same with property investment: you should go in with the attitude that you are going into business. What you buy is important, but so too is managing your properties. You have, at the least, hundreds of thousands of dollars tied up in your properties—you need to look after them and drive them to give you the best return.

When you see your properties as a business, you will realise how important management is and understand the roles that you will have to play. You need to be:

- a marketing manager;
- a customer relationships manager;
- an asset manager;
- a financial officer; and
- a CEO.

Let's go through each of these roles in turn.

Marketing manager

Marketing managers know that they are in competition. They know that tenants have a choice—they can choose your property to rent, or the one down the road. Marketing concerns everything that you have to do with the market—the presentation of the property, how you talk to your customers (which is what your tenants are), whether you make it easy or hard for the tenant to rent and stay in your property—and so on. Marketing managers know that it is far easier and cheaper to retain an existing customer than it is to find a new one. Thus, the marketing manager must keep the pressure on your customer relationships manager.

Customer relationships manager

CRMs know that their job is to keep the customer happy. They know that it is easier (and much more cost effective) to retain existing customers than to find new ones (because the marketing manager has told them that is so). You want to have a low vacancy rate, quite simply because vacancies represent a loss of income. You need to manage your tenants so that they stay with you, just like a business needs to keep customers. This is important to your income and to the value of your property business; a property that has a low vacancy rate is worth more. This might mean doing things to the property to retain tenants—which is where the asset manager's role is important.

Asset manager

This is the person charged with keeping up with maintenance. To fulfil their role properly, asset managers make sure that maintenance and other things are done quickly and efficiently. When the stove does not work, the asset manager gets it fixed quickly because he or she knows that a stove that is not working is a major problem for a tenant. Asset managers build really good relationships with top tradespeople. They do regular checks on the assets they are managing (in this case your properties). They know that when they report to their financial officers, they will be happy because the maintenance work is being done on time, and this costs less in the long run than deferred maintenance.

Financial officer

Financial officers look after the money, making sure that there is enough of it. In fact, they do not want just 'enough'—they want as much as possible. They want to see lots of black numbers on the balance sheet, with lots of zeros on the end, and no red numbers. Financial officers work to keep costs down and income up. That means positive cash flow and high asset values. In particular, your financial officer will work on your borrowings, making sure that any loans you have are the cheapest possible and are structured well. Interest is frequently the biggest cost for property investors and having the right loans is therefore a high priority. Financial officers have the image of being a boring, mean lot. But sometimes they are happy and occasionally they even smile. The thing that makes them happy is when they can report to the CEO that cash flow is strong, asset values are high and all loans are under control. Happiness can be ever so simple.

Chief executive officer

This is you. In fact, you as a property investor have to fill all the above roles but your role as CEO is to make sure that all these jobs are done properly (even if the reality is that *you* do them!). You have to make sure that your strategy is to have a customer-focused property business. In any business, customers are the lifeblood; a property investor's tenants are no different. Tenants should be your prime management focus. You need to make sure your customer relationship manager talks to your asset manager, and that both talk to the financial officer. All of you should talk to the marketing manager so that you are all aware of the strategies that you as CEO have set. Of course this means that you are talking to yourself!

•

Seeing your property investments as a business, and being aware of all the roles that need to be played, is a very good way to organise yourself professionally as a top-notch property investor. As a business owner in the business of property you will make sure that all these roles are performed, and performed well.

Chapter 47 | Shares

You are less likely to become rich through trading and investing in shares than through running a business or investing in property. This is because you need a high level of knowledge to become rich through shares. It is easier to learn what you need to know to become rich through a property portfolio or through running a business. Becoming rich through shares requires you to invest a great deal of time and energy in understanding markets, industries, and individual companies. It also requires continuous monitoring of an aggressive portfolio; you can never relax.

To become rich through shares you will need to invest in them and trade them in a very targeted way. Remember, you are looking for a 15 per cent return after tax, which means beating the market average by quite a long way. The index is an average, it is a portfolio of shares which are weighted in a way so that it can measure the performance of a particular share market. Over time, the index does provide quite good returns, but not at 15% p.a. Your shares therefore have to perform much better than most.

Share traders and serious share investors are very different from the average investor in the share market. To achieve the kind of returns that will make you rich you will need to be:

- **Highly disciplined** Usually you will have your own rules and guidelines for investing and trading and you will stick to them.
- **Committed** To invest and trade for superior returns you will devote a lot of time to watching the markets, managing your portfolio, and educating yourself about what is happening in the industries and companies you are interested in.

- **Tuned in** You will cultivate a network of well-informed people—stockbrokers, businesspeople, other share traders, industry specialists, and so on. You will read widely, study company reports, and attend meetings and seminars.
- **Objective** To be highly successful at share investing and trading you must be able to make rational and logical decisions in the face of the emotional whirlpool that is the share market. You can have no emotional attachment to your portfolio. You must buy and sell with your head, not your heart.

People aiming to become rich through shares usually have two portfolios. The investment portfolio includes the shares that you buy and hold, perhaps for a very long time. Although not actively traded, it will still be quite an aggressive undiversified portfolio, aiming to get 15% p.a. or better. As such, it is still part of Wealth-creating Assets, not Security Assets. The other portfolio, usually smaller in value, contains the shares that you actively trade.

Your investment portfolio will contain shares in a small number of very carefully chosen companies. Many of these companies will be small and you will look to buy early and well and to hold for the long term. You will be looking for growth stocks and seeking to achieve well above the average return. Returns in the form of dividends should be reinvested. Early investors in growth companies have seen such a strategy work very well.

Active share investors seeking to become rich through shares have to look for returns in excess of 15% p.a. from both their investment and trading portfolios.

Chapter 48 | The investment approach

Simply put, for the investment approach to work you are looking to buy shares in a good company, in a good industry, in a good economy. This requires a great deal of work. You will soon find that everything that happens in the world is of interest—political and economic movement, social change, demographic shifts, technological innovations, even the weather! Once you have found a good company you hold it for very long periods (years, even decades in some cases).

To beat the market you will have to buy shares in just a few companies, not a wide spread. You have to pick winners. This entails much more risk than simply investing in an index of shares or buying through a mutual fund. Investing and trading in shares in order to become rich will mean some or all of the following:

- **Buying shares that are not in the index** This is often because the companies are very small. Small companies as a group offer good returns but carry more risk.
- **Buying start-up companies** Again, the risks are high but the returns can also be very good.
- **Buying only a small number of companies** The lack of diversification raises your risk; however, if you pick the right companies you will also outperform the average.

A skilled investor will have shares in fewer companies, most of which will be smaller companies. They often restrict themselves to just a few industries, ensuring that they understand those industries and companies very well. This is opposite to the advice we would give to an unskilled investor who is looking to store wealth and seeking average returns only. (They should have a diversified portfolio, perhaps tracking an index or through a mutual fund.) While the skilled investor is taking more risk, that risk is mitigated by their expertise.

Good share investors have the same attitude as the owner of a business. They treat the companies they are investing as if they owned the whole of each one (instead of just a share of it). Before buying they do thorough due diligence (full scrutiny of all aspects of a business including its finances) and seek to know everything they can about the industry and that business in particular. Disciplined investors seek to satisfy themselves about:

- company performance;
- growth in profit;
- asset quality;
- management acumen;
- opportunities;
- brands, patents, licences, etc.;
- threats; and
- competition.

Good share investors are largely unconcerned with the market; they are focused on the trends in national economies, certain industries and in specific businesses. They are seeking to buy value and to hold the shares. While you cannot afford to forget about any share you have bought, if you make good choices you will be unlikely to buy and sell often. A good discipline is to approach the purchase of any shares you are considering adding to your investment portfolio as if you are buying the entire company.

Successful investors seek value. In short, they look for companies that will deliver sustained and growing profits for years. Whether these profits are paid out as dividends or retained is in most cases immaterial; either you receive income that can be reinvested or the retained earnings will drive up the share values. Sustainable and growing profits are the key to value investing; all you are concerned about is determining how likely those profits are and how much you should pay for a share of them. In brief, this means deciding whether the P:E (or price to earnings ratio) that you calculate for the share is worth the investment.

Chapter 49 | Share trading

Share traders, as opposed to share investors, are interested in buying and selling within shorter timeframes. They are looking for opportunities to take advantage of discontinuities in the market such as stagging (buying new listings intending to on-sell immediately), timing anomalies and special events (including likely restructurings and takeovers). Even more than skilled investors, share traders must be well informed and alert. Speed is of the essence, you will not have the luxury of a 'hold' position if you wish to make money by trading. Thus share traders have to be sufficiently 'up with the play' to take a position and act decisively. A trader's entire portfolio is always for sale, all you are ever thinking about is price.

Share traders choose to trade in busy (or 'thick') markets, for a key feature of their success is the ability to enter and exit rapidly. That is not possible in 'thin' markets where shares are infrequently traded—you can't sell out if no-one is buying!

Your trading portfolio will be smaller in terms of number of shares and total value but more aggressive. You will be acutely aware of the pros and cons of every trade. You will cut your losses ruthlessly. There is no room for emotion in a trading portfolio—poor decisions are not fixed by further poor decisions. The shares that you trade in are simply a commodity, to be bought and sold without any consideration but profit.

The three main areas that provide opportunities for traders are:

- stagging new listings;
- timing the market; and
- special situations.

'Stagging new listings'

This refers to buying an allocation of shares in every company that is newly offered to the public and selling them as soon as they are listed on the sharemarket. Nearly every company that sells shares to the public and subsequently lists comes onto the market above the issue price. As a trader you can take advantage of this; you won't always win but the odds are in your favour. Some initial public offerings (IPOs) are worth holding on to, but that is a judgment you will have to learn to make. Your network matters here—many IPOs are available only through brokers and you will need a good relationship with your broker to get an allocation.

Timing the market

This is more difficult than stagging. Here you are trying to buy low and sell high, just like everyone else. This requires watching the market carefully at all times and being ready to take advantage of only small short-term shift. If you trade frequently, small price discrepancies can amount to considerable profit over time. Take care not to be too greedy, however—it's rarely worth waiting for the last cent. If you are going to attempt to time the market you will pay a lot of attention to moving averages of a company's share price. Again, this information is available to everyone, so you will have to continue to focus on developing your judgment.

Special situations

Active share traders who seek out special situations are looking for companies that are likely to be taken over, companies which have good net assets, but are currently undervalued by the market. There are usually good profits to be made in the short term when a takeover is imminent.

•

Successful share traders set value limits and rules for their trading in four areas:

- **Buy price** Be clear in advance about the price you are prepared to pay. Share trading as opposed to investing is very sensitive to the purchase price.
- **Sell price** Good traders decide in advance at what level they will get out. Most will seek a 10–20 per cent profit, disciplining themselves to take it rather than hold out for the last cent.
- **Stop-loss limit** Good traders protect themselves by specifying a level of loss at which they will sell out. This protects them from losses that are too serious. Left alone, human nature tends to compound poor decisions. Deciding in advance at what level of loss you trigger a sale protects you from the effects of emotional attachment—and stubbornness.
- **Single-trade level** Good traders protect themselves from over-optimism by setting a limit on a single trade—to either a dollar amount, say $20 000, or a percentage, say no more than 30 per cent of their trading funds.

These self-imposed 'rules' can protect the trader's position to a large degree. While it is probably inevitable that they will be broken from time to time, they provide some useful guidelines.

•

If you can apply yourself to share trading you can certainly make money. But to increase returns, really top operators think about gearing for shares.

Chapter 50 | Gearing for shares

Gearing is a way of getting rich faster through shares. It is also a quick way to lose a lot of money. Gearing increases the stakes—both your good decisions and your bad judgments are compounded and magnified many times over.

Skilled investors and traders often use gearing to accelerate their success. They may simply borrow to buy more shares, using the shares they already own as security. This is little different to borrowing to buy property with the bank taking a mortgage over the property as security. It is riskier, however, as the value of a property is much less likely to slump than the value of shares. Shares are much more volatile than property. Skilled investors and traders confident enough to back their own judgment gear using a variety of means, a few of them quite sophisticated. Some methods of gearing even protect capital and limit the downside risk.

Timing is everything when you gear for shares. The money is often borrowed short term, so you are very exposed if a downshift in the market occurs, even if it does not last for very long.

While a bank will lend you money to invest in shares, it won't be as generous with either the amount of money or the interest rate as it would be if you were buying property. There are other, easier ways of gearing for shares, such as buying endowment warrants, using a margin trading facility, or purchasing warrants or options.

Endowment warrants

These are based on buying into a basket of blue chip shares, gearing, and holding for several years. Typically, the investor outlays 50 per cent of the purchase price with the balance provided by the bank. The dividends pay at least a part of the interest of the loan. Almost always, a basket of shares held over a 10-year period will rise in value. At the end of the period you exercise your warrant—the shares are sold, the remainder of your debt is paid and you get a cheque for the balance.

Margin trading

This is the classic way to borrow for shares. The brokerage firm or financial institution will lend you money to buy shares with a deposit (20–50 per cent) from you. Your deposit is called a 'margin', and the relative proportion of your margin to the lender's financing of the shares has to be maintained at all times. It is in effect the lender's 'margin for safety'. The shares are held in the lender's name as security. If the value of the shares falls significantly you will get a 'margin call' from the lender to restore the relative financing. If you cannot meet this call (you don't have the cash) they will sell the shares immediately. You carry almost all of the risk, and you win only if the value of the shares rises. Having your shares lose value is never pleasant but it can be disastrous if you are margin trading. On the other hand, you can also make super profits in this way—using other people's money.

Warrants

Warrants allow you to gear with relatively low risk. They are based around individual shares and give you the right to purchase those shares for a particular price at some time in the future. There is no obligation to buy at that price in the future, which means your risk is limited to what you paid for the warrant.

In this way you have control of a large parcel of shares for relatively little outlay but the risk to you is limited if you have bet wrongly. Warrants can be traded. If the value of the shares rises so too does the value of your warrant, and you may well make a lot of money trading warrants without ever owning a share. The converse, of course, is that the shares do not rise, in which case your warrants go in the rubbish tin!

Options

Call options are very similar to warrants. Put options work in reverse—they give you the right to sell a share for a specified price on a specified date. You are betting on the share value falling—on the due date you will buy the share at the new low value and require the other party to purchase it from you at the higher price of the put option. Again, put options are traded and you don't ever have to deal with the shares themselves.

•

Intelligent gearing is a great way to become rich through shares. You do need to know what you are doing, but when you get it right, gearing will not only allow you to beat the market but will also greatly accelerate your wealth creation.

Part VII

Financial freedom: What it takes

Chapter 51 | Have you got what it takes?

Whatever the starting point, yes—you have got what it takes. Nearly everyone does. There are no natural impediments to becoming wealthy. You do not need to be an academic high achiever, to have gone to the right school or even have money now (although it does help). Everyone can do the things that are necessary to become wealthy—we all have what it takes!

However, the question is probably the wrong one. It should really be: 'Are you prepared to **do** what it takes?'

And the answer here for some people (in fact, for most people) is: 'No!'

There has to be a *desire* to reach financial freedom. This sounds easy enough: surely everyone wants to have enough money to be financially free? Surely everyone wants to be rich?

Well, yes, they do, but in our experience most people do not want it enough. As we said in Chapter 9, to achieve financial freedom, your dream of financial freedom, and your desire for it, must be strong enough to overcome the barriers that you will inevitably encounter.

Nearly everyone wants to be 'rich and free'. But for many it is only a daydream; their dream is not firm enough or they do not want it strongly enough to actually do something about it. What stops most people is not a lack of financial skills (these can be learned), nor a lack of capital (nearly all wealthy people have started with nothing), but the inability to move out of their comfort zone, a reluctance to make the necessary changes and do the hard stuff.

In our experience, these attitudinal or psychological attributes are more important than anything else. We call them the 'soft skills' of wealth, the 'hard skills' being more the technical money stuff. Becoming rich and free requires a certain mindset and attitude, and the self-leadership and energy to make difficult decisions and new choices. Anyone *can* do this—we have seen some of our clients make extraordinary transformations. Few *will* do it—most people's goals and aspirations are too weak or set too low to inspire them to change. Our experience is that it is easy to learn what you need to know to become rich and free if you are willing to make the *choice* to do so. Our clients have found it surprisingly easy to prosper when, and *only* when, they have taken the big decision to do so.

In order to get rich and stay rich, you are going to have to change many of your habits and behaviours. It would be silly to expect this to be easy initially—habits are always hard to break. In time, however, with the right attitude, new habits replace the old ones, and success breeds success. What it takes is the initial commitment to consciously change until new behaviours become habitual.

Many people have to overcome a set of beliefs about money and achievement that they have carried since childhood—self-talk which actively works against becoming rich and free. The tape they are playing in their heads is negative and self-defeating—they have to eject it and put a new one on the deck.

You are going to have to do some hard stuff. Most people shy away from dealing with the difficult decisions. This is especially true when it involves sensitive discussions with family members about expenditure, lifestyle and habits. The rich and free do not avoid these issues (it is one of the things that sets them apart). If you want financial freedom, you have to *face* issues and *fix* them.

Weekly wages and monthly salaries encourage people to live and think in the short term; many people live hand to mouth. To become rich and free, you have to have a different timeframe. You have to consider the longer term and delay gratification (investing for the future rather than spending for today's pleasures), a huge shift in attitude for many people.

If you are unhappy about the state of your finances, then you have to own up to yourself that what you have been doing has not worked. If you are not growing your wealth as fast as you hope or expect, if money seems to slip through your fingers or your investments have not worked out, you need to make new choices and change both your thinking patterns and your daily behaviour.

•

Nothing will stop you other than yourself. Have you got what it takes? Yes! The remainder of this section deals with the challenges you will face and makes suggestions to help you triumph. Remember, anyone can do this—if they want to!

Chapter 52 | Accept change

It is hard to change the habits of a lifetime. It is hard to move out from the comfort of where you are now. But if you are still a long way from having financial freedom, that is what you will have to do. The things that you are doing now have not got you to financial freedom, so you will have to do some things that are different.

You will have to change what you own and what you earn. You will have to change what you know. You need the 'hard skills' of finance—things like knowing about P:E ratios, capitalisation rates, discounted cash flows, the use of a revolving credit facility, the valuation of bonds, synthetic financial instruments, and so on.

These things are relatively easy. The hard skills can be learnt from books or seminars, educational courses, the Net—all the knowledge and material you will require is readily available.

The hard skills are not usually the problem. It is the 'soft skills' that are harder to grasp, things like your attitude and your motivation, keeping the dream in front of you all of the time, setting goals, taking time to plan, developing the determination to keep on going when things get tough. Above all, perhaps you have to learn to find the courage to get started.

Most people learn some of the hard skills—how to buy the right house, how to mortgage the house well, how to pay off the loan and how to invest safely. These are all relatively easy. The people who learn some of the hard skills get ahead of the pack—but they don't get financial freedom. They get security at a modest level.

You are not 'most people' if you have read this far. You are keen on the idea of financial freedom; perhaps you are determined to have it. So you are going to have to do things that are completely outside what most people do if you want not just to be ahead of the pack, but well out in front. Some of those things will be hard. You may need to sell your house and put the money into the business you want to build; you may need to stop those holidays on the Gold Coast that you have taken for the past five years; you may have to convince your partner that the idea of financial freedom in ten years is possible; you may have to fire your accountant, tell the kids they cannot have a PlayStation, deal with difficult tenants and work 60 hours a week. Some of the things that you have to do will seem quite outlandish to most people. You may have to be outlandish—you will certainly have to be different. You will have to do the things that most people won't do.

None of these things require the hard skills of finance. Those hard skills are completely necessary, but they are a lot easier to acquire than the softer skills of attitude and motivation.

The thing that you are really going to have to change is your attitude. Your attitude to risk is the key.

Chapter 53 | Accept risk

There is no escaping it—to become financially free you are going to have to take some risks. You cannot get 15 per cent from your Wealth-creating Assets without some risk, and often those risks will be quite high. You have to face the fact that nearly everyone who becomes wealthy takes risks to get there.

Different people respond to risk in different ways. At one end of the spectrum are those who actually like risk. They get a buzz from it; for them risk is like an addiction. They play the markets, often all the markets, in a haphazard way. Others will not accept any risk at all; government bonds and cash at the bank are acceptable, but not much else.

Neither group is likely to achieve financial freedom. The ones who are addicted to risk will keep on playing the game with ever-increasing stakes until they come unstuck (and when they do come unstuck they do so quite spectacularly). Those who will not take risks, on the other hand, will do nothing useful towards financial freedom. (As Shakespeare said, 'Nothing will come of nothing.')

The right approach is different: it is feeling the fear, but doing it anyway. Know that what you are doing has higher risks, but know that you have to do it if you are going to reach your goals. Embrace risk, even welcome it, as an inevitable part of getting rich. But you must respect it as well: the issue is not avoiding risk but managing it. Risk and return are linked—to get high returns you incur higher risk. The greater the returns you are seeking the better you will need to learn to manage the risk.

Some risks are quite obvious: your business may fail; your properties may not perform well and the bank calls in your loan; the share market may crash. Because your Wealth-creating Assets are not going to be diversified, and you have a lot riding on them, the chances of a failure over the next ten years are high. The trick is to make sure that any failures are not fatal.

The risks that you will take can be managed to some extent in two important ways:

- **Continually analysing what you are doing** Take your time to really think about what you are proposing to do, discuss it with your partner and your professional advisors. There is usually no hurry—if you miss an opportunity because you have thought about it for too long, don't worry; there are always more opportunities out there.
- **Continually siphoning off some of your wealth into Security Assets** This is your fallback position. It will mean that your wealth does not grow quite as quickly, but you have something behind you if things turn bad.

Perhaps the greatest risk is less about money and more about time. You risk giving up a decade or two of your life, giving up a fair bit of the lifestyle that you had (you may have sold the boat!), and it may not work out. Time is any investor's or business owner's greatest asset. If you try and fail you will probably end up about where you started. Perhaps you have not lost much money, but you have lost time. You can get any monetary loss back, but you cannot regain the time.

However, that risk of time lost has to be balanced against the risk of doing nothing. Looking back with regret at what might have been is perhaps the worst thing that could happen—better to have tried and failed than not to have tried at all. People who avoid all risk pay the biggest price of all—they never act on their dreams. They have to live with the constant thought of what might have been. It's a big price to pay for being completely risk-averse.

We cannot find a way to financial freedom that is completely without risk. We try to reduce risk for our clients, but ultimately you have to back your decisions with your money. Again, timeframes are important. Often when people come unstuck in their wealth-creating activities it is because they have not come to terms with their own emotional responses to risk. Too often we see people buying at the top of the market and selling at the bottom because their emotional response to risk is overriding their head and their hand. Running a business, investing in property, managing a share portfolio, all carry risks. Understanding and accepting risk, and making sound well-founded decisions, are requirements for success. Abandoning your investments at the first sign of risk is disastrous; likewise, emotional attachment to wrong decisions in the face of all the facts is ruinous.

The game of financial freedom is singles. In the final analysis, you are on your own and your final position will depend on the judgments that *you* make. You can have all the advisers and experts that you want, along with a great network, but ultimately, whatever you do will be your decision.

Nurturing your dream will give you the fortitude to take and live with these risks. That clearly defined dream lets you do the hard stuff. And the hard stuff includes taking on risk.

Chapter 54 | Nurture the dream

You can have financial freedom—provided that you have a compelling dream and believe that you can do it. We have already talked about your dream and its importance in Chapters 8 and 9. This is not a bad time to go back and read it again.

Note that the dream has to be about a way of life, not about a particular amount of money. Getting rich and staying rich is about delivering your dream—the money is a vehicle for your dream, not an end in itself. Money is only important for what you will be able to do with your life when you have it. No one would so much as get out of bed for $1 million (or $100 million for that matter) if the money did not let them do the things that they wanted to do.

You have to truly *believe* in the dream, and know that you *can* have financial freedom. You have to do a sales job on yourself and continually sell yourself the dream. You have to believe that your dream is good and worthy and is something that you want to buy into. You have to sell yourself the features, advantages and benefits to *you* of financial freedom and show yourself that the cost is in fact good value. If your dream is not big enough, not worthy of such commitment, then now is a good time to think it through some more. You are worth a big dream—keep working on it until it is worthy of you.

You may also have to sell the vision to your partner; he or she has to buy into a dream as well. The first rule of sales is to believe in the product; to encourage your partner to share a dream you have to believe in it (even love it) so strongly that you can sell it. Sometimes we find that one partner has done much more thinking than the other about a dream. These couples need to allow time to catch up with each other, to harmonise and build a shared dream. A person will rarely follow someone else's dream—your dream must become your partner's dream. While your energy will be inspiring to your partner, you need to allow time to build a shared vision of the future. It will take the focus and commitment of both partners to realise your goals so you both need to be fully enrolled in the dream. You will need each other's support along the way and be able to keep reminding each other why you are making all the changes that you are making. Thus both of you must have no doubts that the dream is good and achievable, the right thing to do with your lives. Keep believing in the dream so that you can keep on selling it to yourselves. Talk about your dream to each other as much as possible. Without this, at any point in time one of you may falter.

Be careful about sharing your vision with anyone else but your partner. If you make the mistake of telling a lot of people about what you are setting out to do, you will have a lot of knockers. Whether they are motivated by envy or something else, the knockers will heap scorn on you. We think that it is best to keep your dreams, goals and plans to yourself—when you encounter knockers you need a lot more self-belief to withstand them and put up with their jibes. Setting out to make your dreams come true can look very threatening to family and friends—as can all achievement above the average. People often respond very negatively to those in their circle who are making positive changes in their lives.

Chapter 55 | Leave your 'buts' behind

People say to us: 'Yes, I would like to be financially free, BUT I don't have enough money to start with' or 'Yes, that would be good, BUT it might not work out and I might become poor.'

Forget the 'buts'! The only impediments to becoming financially free are within. You are no more disadvantaged than anyone else. Lots of people start with nothing, and lots of people succeed against the odds.

People usually worry needlessly; sometimes they are not even sure what they are worrying about. Worry is the biggest impediment to getting on and becoming financially free. Studies have shown that:

- 40 per cent of worry is about things that will never happen;
- 30 per cent of worry is about things that cannot be changed;
- 12 per cent of worry is about health; and
- 8 per cent of worry is about petty little things of no account.

That leaves 10 per cent of worry. Define what those real worries are, then deal with them. Make a plan so that if the thing you are worrying about does become true, you can fix it. Certainly there are risks, things that you *should* worry about. These need to be clearly defined so that you can ignore the things you can do nothing about and get on with managing the things you can do something about.

The impediments to achieving financial freedom are in your mind. It is negative thoughts that are stopping you. Negative thoughts are powerful—they can stop you getting started, or once you have started can stop you carrying through with your plans. Yes, there are real worries, but remember that change can create feelings and thoughts of vague, undefined disease. The real worries must be dealt with; the others must be banished before you are disabled by them.

Thoughts are powerful—they define what you do and what you will become in a process that works like this: your thoughts determine your actions; those actions become habits; your habits are who you become.

There is plenty of evidence that people are more sensitive to the idea of any kind of loss than they are to gain. Think about it. This means we are so sensitive to losing money that we would choose to do nothing to gain financial freedom rather than take the risk of loss!

Drag out all your buts and examine them. Are they really good reasons for denying yourself the opportunity to be rich and free? Isn't your dream worth challenging these buts? Which buts are real, and which are just undefined fear of change?

Ultimately, everyone who wants to be rich and free will have to get off their buts.

Chapter 56 | The 'but' of age

You can always find an excuse for not becoming financially free. If you are running low on excuses for not acting you can always blame your age. This is the biggest 'but', the biggest and most common excuse for lack of action that we hear. It is an easy excuse that can be hauled out and used by anyone at any time:

- From age 18 to 24 you can always say that there is plenty of time and you'll get onto it soon (and buy a lottery ticket).
- From age 25 to 49 you can always say that you are too busy with the kids, the mortgage and the job (and buy a lottery ticket).
- Over age 50 you can simply say that it is too late (and buy a lottery ticket).

We have our own but to answer the but of age: *but* what happens if you *don't* win the lottery?

The truth is that it's never too soon and it's never too late! The but of age is the most spurious and irrelevant excuse of all. Use it if you want to, but when people use it to us we know that it is not real and that there is something else which is really applying the brakes.

Time really does matter when you are working to become rich and free. In fact, in growing wealth, time is your very best friend. That is because of the effect of compounding—the growth of money and assets invested over time. More about that later. However, no matter what age you are, you should begin. Young people usually have very little money but they have the enormous advantage of years of compounding on their side. Those who are extremely busy with careers and children have large outgoings and feel they have little to spare. However, these are usually their years of highest income potential and it is a great time to make smart decisions about investments for creating wealth and building security. Older people have less of a time advantage but usually have more income and assets (on which they are often getting very little return) and greater experience and self-knowledge. Better decisions will make a big difference: older people often know more and have better self-mastery to help them in getting the outcomes they want.

Many people have a very self-limiting approach to age. Life expectancy is longer than ever before in history. In addition, we can expect to be active and healthy for much longer. Are you making your horizons too short? What's your mental use-by date? If you knew you were going to live to be 100 or you knew that you would be active and healthy until you were in your nineties, would you think differently about planning and investing in order to be rich and free for the several decades to come?

Whatever age and stage you are at, *now* is the time to start! When it comes to generating wealth, starting early and young is the most controllable strategy. You are never going to get any younger—*now* is the earliest you can start.

Chapter 57 | What's your baggage?

If any of your thoughts about financial freedom are negative you are unlikely to achieve your goals because you will keep getting in your own way. When your thinking and your self-talk are positive, you have a lot of power to support yourself on your journey to financial freedom. You can change. This starts with your thoughts.

The most common negative thoughts about financial freedom include:

- **Money is 'not nice'** Somehow there is a feeling that it is not nice to be wealthy, that by having a lot you are taking away from others. This is nonsense—wealth is not a zero-sum game. If you become wealthy, you do not take that wealth away from someone else—chances are you are making someone else's life better. Few people become financially free without enriching others. Growing wealth is a win-win game. An economy is not a closed system—it is open and growing.
- **Loss aversion** This is a reasonable worry and one that you can at least take some steps to avert. However, to become financially free you have to face the fact that you will have to take some risks. The real loss for most people lies in never attempting to achieve their dreams. Nothing ventured, nothing gained.
- **Regret or wishing you had done it sooner** The answer to this one is obvious—do you want to keep on regretting it, or get on with it? Your regret will not stop until you make a start. People have a tendency to compound bad decisions—rather than admit to being wrong, we tend to insist on continuing to be wrong! We value consistency too highly at

times—we all want to be thought of as behaving consistently, and making changes means being inconsistent. Better to change and be inconsistent!

- **No money to start with** Well, you have to make a start somewhere, or you will continue to have nothing. Most of the world's wealthy started with nothing—that is the natural state. Nearly everyone has enough income over the course of the years to make becoming financially free possible. If you have the commitment you have more than most to begin with.
- **The 'at 65' mentality** This is the idea that you will retire at 65 years and enjoy your retirement with what the government gives you. First, the government is not going to give you very much. Second, why wait for that long to enjoy life? Third, there is a great deal of living to do in the decades beyond 65!
- **I am comfortable and I am enjoying life now as it is** Great! Keep on doing it. If this response is true, we have no argument with it. (But then why are you reading this book?)

All these thought patterns can stop you pursuing financial freedom. However, all but the last can be overcome—and the last one does not need to be overcome if that is what you truly believe. Think about what your concerns are. Work out which are real and which are just an excuse for not getting out of your comfort zone.

Many people's heads are also filled with unhelpful messages and myths about money that they picked up from their home and school. Amongst the least helpful are:

- You have to have money to make money.
- You have to be highly intelligent to make money.
- You have to have a good education to make money.
- Our family has never been any 'good' at money.
- Money is the root of all evil.

You may need to write down all the negative messages you are carrying in your head about money and examine them one by one. Our early conditioning, especially from people like parents and teachers, is very powerful. None of the above messages is true, of course—unless you choose to believe them! Whatever you believe will be true for you.

What we tell ourselves is very important in influencing our success or failure. Listen to the tapes you are playing in your head and change them to better messages if you need to. Watch your language! When we use phrases like 'filthy rich' or comments like 'money is the root of all evil' we sabotage our efforts to become financially free. Being rich and free is neither 'evil' nor 'filthy'. To the contrary, it is in yours and everyone else's interest that you become rich and free.

Chapter 58 | Doing the hard stuff: Eat up your frogs

There is a technique we advocate for helping you with some of the hard stuff that comes originally from Mark Twain. It is a technique for those who procrastinate, putting off the difficult things that we all have to do from time to time. Putting off an unpleasant task is a natural human response. However, there are some hard things that you simply have to do if you are going to achieve your goals.

Mark Twain's thoughts to stop procrastination went like this: Imagine that you have to (yes, absolutely have to) eat a live, large, slimy green frog. You have no choice about this—you have to do it.

When are you going to do it? Are you going to leave it sitting on your desk (or kitchen table) watching you while you contemplate every disgusting mouthful? Are you going to leave it there for a few days or weeks while you 'think' about it?

Or are you going to get on with it, eat it now and get the unpleasantness over with?

The answer is to get on with it: there is no point in waiting because you are going to have to do it. Surely it is better to eat it now and stop the thing looking at you like that. It will not taste any more pleasant in a few days (conceivably quite a lot worse!). Doing it now, you have the same nasty experience as doing it later—what you do not have is the worry and stress of 'thinking' about doing it. Once you have eaten the frog it no longer sits there staring at you revoltingly. Once you've done it, you've done it—it's over.

Some people are more prone to procrastination than others, although all of us want to put off the hard things for as long as possible. Procrastination serves no purpose, however, the frog (or the problem) is not going to go away. You have to face it and fix it (or in the case of a frog, eat it!).

We often give our clients a large frog (made out of china!) to sit on their desks and serve as a constant reminder to do the hard stuff. This is useful not just for getting started, but for all the ongoing tasks that you do not really want to do (but have to).

Reaching financial freedom will not be just one sweet, easy ride (a few mouthfuls of candy floss); you are going to have to eat some frogs. Whether it is taking on more debt, selling the boat or evicting difficult tenants, there will be some hard stuff. Are you going to do it now, or are you going to wait? You probably know the things that you should be doing, should have done. That you have not done them makes you feel uncomfortable or even guilty. Those unpleasant feelings are going to remain with you until you have fixed the problem, in exactly the same way as the unpleasant contemplation of the prospect of eating a frog will be with you until it has been done.

Make a list of the things that you have been putting off. Identify and define your frogs, face them looking them straight in the eye—and then eat them. Doing the hard stuff is a winning strategy.

Chapter 59 | Learn to think long term

If there is one dominant theme in what we talk about, in how we coach and in this book, it is: you have to make some sacrifices now to achieve something better (a lot better) in the future. Ask yourself how your world will be different in the future as a result of what you choose today. The future that we talk about is unlikely to be tomorrow, however, or the day after. It is likely to be years, even a decade, away. That is hard—people do not want to delay gratification, especially if the delay is for years.

Staying focused on what you are doing over such a long period of time is difficult. It is not just that you may have to go without some of the things that other people have (a nice car, a holiday), but that your plans will only work if they are given time. That requires patience and the ability to focus and concentrate on a goal for a long period. It is easy to lose your way, lose your dream, at some point and wander off into other things.

Over the years while you are running your business, investing in property or shares, there will inevitably be times when you lose confidence in what you are doing, when the plan does not seem to be working at all. Most Wealth-creating Assets are volatile—they do not go up at a nice and neat 15% p.a. month after month, year after year. Your business is quite likely to have a couple of flat years, perhaps followed by a really bad year, and then some real boomers. Property and share markets do much the same.

This means that you have to remain very focused on what it is you are doing, very focused on your vision, your goals, your plan. By all means review the goals and the plan, and change them if they no longer seem right. No matter what happens, however, the *vision* must remain in clear focus throughout—it

; this that will help you overcome the many difficulties you will ace.

When you review what it is that you are doing, try to stand ack and look at the big picture. It may be that you have had couple of ordinary years and over that time you have not ecome wealthier (maybe you have even become less so). Do not eact to setbacks like this immediately. Instead, look at the big icture—is the graph of your net worth overall heading in the ght direction? Looking at the big picture, considering your erformance over years rather than the way things have gone ecently, is the way to override feelings of despondency and lack f confidence. The negative feelings that you will develop from me to time have to be banished by a rational look at the long-erm direction.

Yes, it is hard to stand back and look at the overall direction. is hard to ignore all the reactive short-term comments made y people often styled as experts. It *is* hard to work out what ents will have a real and lasting effect on your position, and hat will not. For example, the markets (and the people who omment on them) get very concerned about the upcoming ection, a higher than expected quarterly inflation figure, the signation of a minister of finance or governor of the Reserve ank, and other such things.

In reality, none of these things is likely to permanently affect ur long-term drive for wealth. Certainly they send a lot of ople into a spin—one adverse balance of payments figure can und in the media like the end of the world. However, you do ot have to join these people, spinning and shouting about the d of the world. Instead, stay focused on what it is you are ing. Yes, an increase in interest rates may make the game a bit rder, but is no reason to get out of the game and do something e. People still make money in tough economic times. Even if u cannot thrive for the moment, you need to hold your position so that when times become good again (as they inevitably will) you are ready to prosper from them.

The game of reaching financial freedom is not won or lost in one parliamentary election or two negative-growth GDP figures. It is a long game, much more of a marathon than a sprint. It needs to be viewed tactically and strategically from far above, so that you can see both the start line and the finish line, and where you are in the race. The important thing is that you get to the finish—what is not important are the side roads and detours you take to get there.

Stand back regularly and make sure that you are on the right track and heading in the right direction. Do not be reactive, jumping from pillar to post because of every little alarm. You knew when you set out for financial freedom that there would be difficulties and setbacks. When they arise, remind yourself that they are expected, they are a part of the process, and keep on playing the game as before.

Chapter 60 | Learn from the masters

You can learn from the people who have already achieved financial freedom. Forget the ones who have stumbled to it, those who have married wealth or inherited it, or been lucky enough to win a lottery. None of these people has gone out to deliberately grasp financial freedom. (And some of them are not so lucky! Research in the United Kingdom suggests that 85 per cent of those who have a major lottery win are back where they started within five years.) These people are not useful models. Look instead at the people who have set out to become wealthy, and succeeded.

We have been thinking, writing and talking about business, success and money for nearly 20 years. Over that time we have met a lot of people who have succeeded, and a lot who have failed. Those who reach financial freedom tend to have a number of things in common (some of which are quite surprising).

- **They are not ego driven** They do not do what they do because they are concerned about what other people might think about them. They are quite happy to invest in unglamorous industries—they do not need to be in airlines or the ski industry. They know there is money in dirt. They are quite happy to go without the toys many of us think are necessary (but which in reality are simply things to make us look good in our own eyes or in the eyes of others).
- **They are not conspicuous in their consumption** They do not live in especially expensive houses nor drive flashy cars—at least, not when they are developing their wealth, and often not even when they have made it.

- **They are independent minded** They do not move with the herd; they are not derailed by talk of recession or international events. This takes courage. They have analysed, they have planned—and they back themselves to be right, even when others think that they are wrong. They listen to others, but in the end they are their own people.
- **They have good long-term relationships and marriages** Whether this is because they are good with people (have a high emotional intelligence) or because their wealth has not been halved by a marriage break-up is uncertain. Nevertheless, it is true that people who are wealthy tend to have good long-term marriages.
- **They know about things like money and tax** The hard skills are a prerequisite, although easier to learn than the soft skills.
- **They take a position** They do not hedge their bets or equivocate. Sometimes this can be a fault—many who get rich do not stay rich.
- **They can see both sides of a situation** They think about what they are going to do, and can see both the pros and the cons of it. In doing so they analyse well and make informed choices. A useful technique here is: before making an important decision, pretend that you have to make the case for *not* doing what you want to do. This forces you to look at both sides of a question.
- **They are persistent** Many have said that they have become 'instantly rich' after 20 years of hard work.
- **They are well connected** This does not mean that they move in the 'right' set or go to the 'right' bars and cafes. These things may be helpful for some people in some business areas, but they are not critical. Rather, it means that they have a good network of contacts in whatever field they are in: top property people know the best real estate agents and valuers; top business people are active in their trade associations; top

share market investors know and talk to several different brokers.

Above all, the two things that set successful people apart are:

- Hard work; and
- Homework.

No-one succeeds without these things. The only lazy ways to riches are to inherit it, steal it, marry it or win it—and these are, respectively, uncertain, risky, possibly not much fun, and even more uncertain!

Although the idea of hard work and homework does not sound particularly joyful, successful people enjoy what they do. They love the share market and are happy to read about it at nights; they love their businesses and are happy to be the first there in the morning and last to leave at night; they are happy to 'work' twelve hours a day because for them it is not really work.

This can be hard on families, however, and some wealthy people do become boring and mean. When people lose the vision they first had of financial freedom (when somewhere along the way money has become an end in itself rather than a means to live the dream), they can lose contact with their partners and families. Your partner must share your vision, plans and goals, and you should be sure that it is always the dream or vision that is important, and not the game itself.

'Work' does not have to be a negative word—lots of people love work. Work for those who are successful is their vocation, hobby and occupation all rolled into one. You are, of course, much more likely to enjoy what you do if you are successful at it. Similarly, you are much more likely to be successful if you enjoy what you do.

•

Becoming financially free is a game—a great game. There is no reason why you cannot play it and win. To get rich and stay rich you have to love what you do and do what you love. Know your dream and love your dream. It is that vision of the future that will set you apart from the herd, let you do things differently and become financially free.

Part | VIII

Stay rich—think security

Chapter 61 | Security

Security is not just a great word—it is a great feeling. As you grow your wealth, and get closer to your dreams, you will have more and more to take care of. Secure your dreams—they should be permanent and sustainable, not simply some all-too-short good times. The real key to financial freedom and realising sustainable dreams is to ensure that your wealth is safe and that your position is unassailable.

You need to take care of what you love by refusing to be like the people who become rich and lose it all again. Such people forget their dream and forget that they are the guardians of what they have created. Their game becomes the building of wealth for its own sake—they are playing with numbers, rather than protecting their own and other people's lives. They become overconfident and believe that their business decisions are impeccable, that property prices will always rise, that their choice of share investments is infallible. The evidence says otherwise. We all have a tendency towards playing double or quits, holding such faith in the choices we have already made that we follow them with more in the same direction. We also have a great need to see ourselves as consistent. While this can compound success it can hugely amplify any errors as well.

Remind yourself of your dreams. Consider again what it is that you love, what you have gone to all this trouble for. Think of the people you love who you want to care for, the life that you want, the things that you love to do. Your task is to make sure that these things are secure—if you love them enough you will not want to put them at risk.

It is very important to start building a portfolio of Security Assets from the very beginning. At best, this means that over the years you accumulate significant wealth in safe assets with a low-risk profile that will give you the passive income you need for financial freedom. At worst, you have a backstop so that if your wealth-creating activities turn sour you will still have some assets and be able to begin over. You also need to think about the ownership of vehicles you are using for both your Wealth-creating and Security Assets, and get your ownership structures right.

Much of the advice in the following chapters is of the 'sensible' variety (which all too often has little appeal for those who are in a great hurry simply to be rich). Our experience of dealing with people who ignore Security Assets suggests that for very little effort and only a small dilution of their wealth-creating ability they could have saved themselves much pain and anguish. Do not let ego get in the way of the security that your dreams and your family deserve. Be sure that the dream is still there, and that you are not doing things simply because you want the numbers on your net worth statement to be bigger.

Remember to split your income so that you build security and can take care of what you love. Depending on what you do this will require different decisions. Those of you who derive your income from a career need to re-evaluate your current consumption, re-evaluate the amount that should be diverted into your wealth-creating activity, and what amount should be diverted into Security Assets. This is always a challenge when habits have to change and there are implications for your lifestyle. However, remember that as you continue to work to the model, further income will be generated through your wealth-creating activities. We recommend that a proportion of this extra income be tagged for diversion into Security Assets. The remainder (after tax) should be invested back in wealth creation.

People who own a business often struggle even more with this diversion of income to Security Assets. They are accustomed to ploughing everything back into the business (and probably don't pay themselves properly either!). It is important to develop the habit of splitting your income from the business into a proportion for reinvestment in the business, a proportion for Security Assets and an agreed amount for consumption. This is the only way to avoid playing double or quits with your business activity. The same is true for those of you who are investing aggressively in shares, or have a highly leveraged property portfolio, or have invested everything in the creation of intellectual property.

Follow your passion by all means. Few people are successful without a devotion to their chosen path. Nevertheless, it is possible to achieve what you are striving for *and* create some security and backstops along the way. It is also possible to structure your affairs and asset ownership so that you protect your assets from unforeseen events. This may mean talking to an accountant or lawyer and paying for their time, but smart operators recognise that this is a key part of the game. Remember the endgame is security, taking care of what you love.

So—right from the beginning of your path to becoming rich and free, you will be planning to divert income into Security Assets. The security effect will be small in the early years, as you will have little in this portfolio. Remember, however, that it grows and compounds in just the same way as the assets in your Wealth-creating Assets portfolio (although not as fast). The other very important effect is the building of a habit—a habit that will ensure that you stay rich!

But first, let's look at how you should structure the ownership of your assets . . .

Chapter 62 | Structuring for asset protection

You can structure asset ownership to enhance your security. One of the important things to realise is that having all your assets—business, family home, portfolio of shares, whatever—in your own name is very risky. If you have a disaster in your business or you are exposed through debt, *all* your assets are at risk.

You should run your Wealth-creating Assets through a limited liability company. This is not perfect as insurance for security or protection, but it does help towards limiting your liability. *You* do not go broke if your company fails unless you have given a personal guarantee (which may be unavoidable for a period at least), or are deemed to have been trading recklessly. A company should give you protection against your trade creditors if the worst happens. Your bank may still be able to get at other family assets through any personal guarantee you have given, but some protection is better than none.

If your Wealth-creating Assets are complicated—for example you have several different businesses or a multi-divisional business—you may need to have the various assets held by separate companies. While this costs more to set up and takes extra time to administer (separate accounts, separate tax returns, separate GST and so on) it can be well worthwhile from a security perspective. If you keep the entities truly separate, with no company owning another, and can avoid giving cross-guarantees, the failure of one of the entities will not affect the others. Successful corporations and entrepreneurs structure their holdings in this way to minimise risk, so that they can 'prune' a dead or dying branch. The ability to lop off one diseased branch without killing the whole tree is a key idea when thinking about asset protection.

Financial affairs have a tendency to become more complicated over time. What may start as a house with a huge mortgage and a small struggling business can eventually become a very complicated portfolio of personal and business assets. You may need specialised advice to get your ownership structured properly, especially in terms of security. This is not an area to scrimp on—you need to get good advice and you will have to pay for it. Your family accountant or lawyer will do the best they can as you build up assets—but if the whole picture is not apparent to them because you have not revealed all your affairs, or they do not realise the long-term implications from a taxation or security point of view, you could one day be in trouble.

You need to sit down with specialist professionals and discuss your concerns about asset protection and security. Many lawyers and accountants report that their clients tell them how well the business is going and how it is beyond imagining that it could ever fail. You need to be different (you are not 'most people'): you need to tell your professionals how well the business is going but that you *can* imagine it failing, and that it is their job to minimise the impact of that failure. If you give your professionals a proper brief they should be able to come up with an asset protection plan that will increase your level of security.

Remember, however, that in the early years at least you will not be able to protect everything completely. At the very least your bank will have a personal guarantee that means that if a company of yours fails and there is a shortfall of what is owed, the bank will be able to get at anything else that you own. In this respect, a personal guarantee acts as a bridge, allowing the lender who has been granted it to cross from one company to another.

You will not be able to stop someone to whom you have given a personal guarantee from getting at everything else that you own. Nor can you stop such a lender when you have given multiple securities—when you have given, as security, assets in a different company from the one that is doing the borrowing. The lender can then move on that security. Lenders who have been granted personal guarantees or multiple securities are very difficult to stop.

Banks aside, there are plenty of other lenders from whom you can and should protect yourself. These are your trade creditors (unsecured creditors), the people from whom you get your monthly supplies (for example, stock if you are in a business). These lenders usually have no guarantee from you, nor any security (although they may have retained ownership of what they have supplied, which would allow them to take possession if their bill is not paid).

A company can give quite good protection against trade creditors—the supplier has supplied and given credit to your company, not to you personally. Thus if the company does fail, it is the *company* that owes the supplier, not you. The trade creditor cannot move on anything else that you own. There can be an exception to this whereby unsecured creditors can get at other assets that you own. This applies to people with a lot of assets and a number of different companies who have not structured their companies well.

It may be that you each have property in a separate company, or groups of properties in separate companies, or different divisions of your business in separate companies. Whatever the case, the structure of ownership is very important. There are two ways of owning companies:

- a chain of companies (the *wrong* way); and
- a 'hub and spokes' of companies (the *right* way).

Chain of companies

This is a structure where one company owns another as a subsidiary, which in turn owns another, and so on, to form a chain.

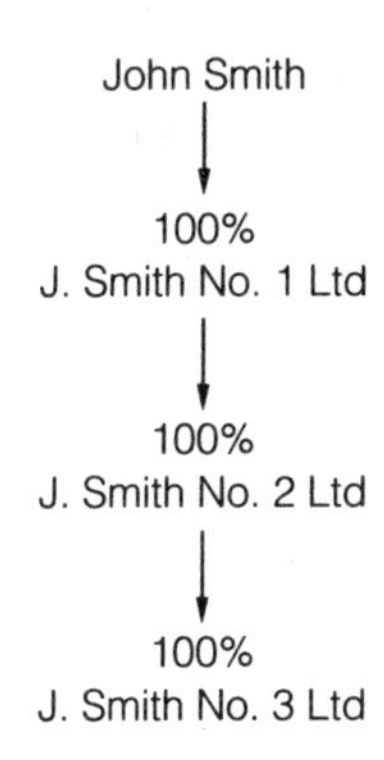

Each company thus owns another as a subsidiary. The problem is that if one of them fails, it can take with it some or all of the others that are further down the chain. This is because whatever a company owns is an asset of that company and is therefore available to creditors (even those without personal guarantees). In this example, imagine that J. Smith No. 1 Ltd went into liquidation. The liquidator would need to recover as much as possible for creditors and so would take control of all assets. One of those assets is 100 per cent of the shares of J. Smith No. 2 Ltd, thus the liquidator would have control of all the assets of J. Smith No. 2 Ltd. Amongst the assets of J. Smith No. 2 Ltd are all the shares of J. Smith No. 3 Ltd, so the liquidator now has control of this company as well.

Because of this chain-like structure, the liquidator is able to get control of (and ultimately sell) all the J. Smith companies. This is the domino effect—one fallen company can knock the others over! This is a very poor structure for asset protection purposes.

Hub and spoke companies

This is an arrangement in which there is one company in the centre (the hub) that owns each of the companies in the group.

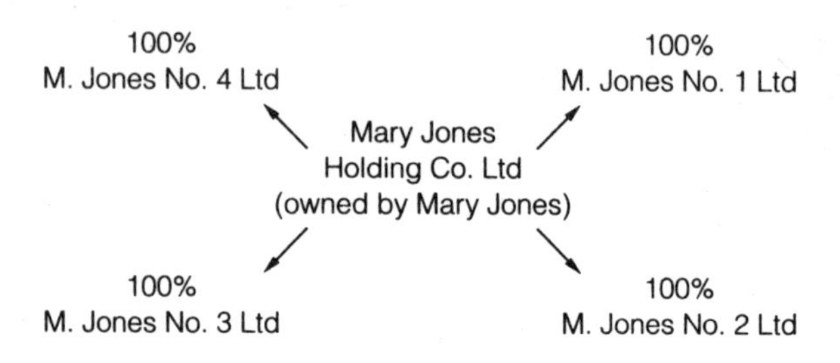

A structure like this means that if M. Jones No. 2 Ltd goes into liquidation, none of the other companies is directly affected. M. Jones No. 2 Ltd can be cut off like the dead branch of a tree without the rest of the tree being affected.

This hub and spoke structure is the best form for asset protection purposes. It will not, however, protect against a bank or anyone else with a personal guarantee. If one of the companies fails, a lender with a personal guarantee will still be able to get at all the companies that you own. For example, if M. Jones No. 2 Ltd failed and there was a shortfall to a bank that held a personal guarantee, the bank could get at all of Mary Jones' other assets. These other assets include the holding company and the assets of the holding company—which include the shares it owns in various other M. Jones companies.

However, while there may be no protection from the bank under this structure, there is protection from trade creditors. In our experience, the bank is very often not the biggest problem when it comes to insolvency. Banks have usually made their loans so that they are fairly sure they will get paid. In particular, having taken security over property and other company assets means they will get paid in priority to others. The bank very often gets paid in full from the failed company's assets—you can't really protect from them. It is the trade creditors who do not get paid that you really need protection from—and intelligent ownership structures can do that.

Chapter 63 | Ownership of Security Assets

You need to think hard about how you structure your business or property assets (your Wealth-creating Assets). You need to think just as hard about the ownership vehicles and structures for your Security Assets.

Your Security Assets should be kept separate from your Wealth-creating Assets, as far as possible being quarantined off or isolated from your more risky assets. Being smart about this will mean that you do not keep your store of wealth mixed up with, and owned by, the entity that owns your business or property investments. This means setting up a separate company or trust to own your Security Assets—unfortunately, more expense and more ongoing management, but necessary all the same. The cost of establishing and continuing to manage a separate company or trust for ownership of your passive investments is well worthwhile from a security point of view.

Our preferred vehicle for ownership of Security Assets is usually a trust. This is because a trust is not 'owned' by you like a company is and therefore has the effect of putting a firewall between your Wealth-creating Assets and your Security Assets, isolating them from each other. Well-designed trust arrangements provide the best form of asset protection and are used by those in the know in just about every country in the world. That said, trusts do not work for everyone in all circumstances. This is for four reasons:

- Trusts can be expensive to set up and manage. If you are at the start of the road to financial freedom you may not have enough assets to justify this cost.
- There is a loss of control when assets go into a trust. You will no longer own the assets in the trust (the trustees do), and

even though you will expect to have use of the assets, you are to some extent reliant on the trustees.

- You may find that an asset like the family home that was previously exempt from capitals gains tax becomes subject to CGT because it cannot be the 'principal residence' of a trust. If the family home does not go into a trust with your other investments, it will probably stay in your own name.
- A trust needs to be set up early and any gifting to be done must be completed well before there is any problem.

If these four things conspire against your use of a trust, you may want to own your Security Assets in a company. This will not give you as much protection—the shares will still be in your name, are an asset of yours, and are therefore not quarantined as they would be in a family trust. However, owning Security Assets in a company does at least have the effect of keeping them separate in your mind. Holding your diversified portfolio of safe investments in a company forces you to see them as separate. They are in a different box or compartment, they have a different purpose from other things that you own and will therefore be managed differently, always with a view to storing wealth instead of creating it. Having your safe investments in a separate company should continually remind you of their 'separateness', and maybe help you resist the temptation to one day use your Security Assets for some risky play.

Ideally, your Security Assets should be protected and isolated to such an extent that if you failed completely and were legally judged bankrupt, they would still be available for your and your family's use. This may sound like a fairly extreme scenario, but there are plenty of cases of high profile, previously high net worth individuals who have gone bankrupt but whose lifestyle has never really changed—they have continued to live in the same houses, drive the same cars and their consumption of Dom Perignon has not changed. This is largely because they used trusts to shelter assets from creditors.

Chapter 64 | What works as a Security Asset?

Security Assets are, by definition, investments that are relatively safe. This means things that are lower risk and therefore have lower returns. The risk/return equation is immutable; the higher the expected return from an investment, the higher the risk. Security Assets need to be at the lower end of the risk spectrum and therefore will give lower returns. You should not be bothered by this because the money that you have in Wealth-creating Assets should be working hard; you can afford to have your money in Security Assets just ticking over.

Many people who have committed to growing their wealth and are on the way to becoming rich resent the idea of diverting any money into assets which do not give high returns. Returns of 15 per cent and above can be very intoxicating and people are often reluctant to slow their journey to riches by putting some of their wealth into Security Assets. They succumb to the temptation to put funds into high-risk investments. In doing so they fulfil part of the reason for having Security Assets—they have got some money out of their wealth-creating activity; they have stopped playing double or quits and diversified somewhat. But putting funds into high-risk investments means they do not have a reliable store of wealth, funds that they can expect to be available when they need them. They do not have something that will give them a safe passive income that will allow them to enjoy freedom.

People like this are almost addicted to the art of the deal. They feel a deep need to chase high returns using the money that is meant to be held safe and secure makes little sense, but they 'have' to be into everything that is going (and often end up going with nothing). Chasing high returns successfully requires focus and concentration—focus that should be concentrated on your Wealth-creating Asset. Security Assets ought not to require this degree of attention.

Bearing this in mind, your three principal Security Assets will be:

- the family home;
- a diversified portfolio; and
- un-geared, top-quality investment property.

You will manage your Security Assets division like 'most people' manage their total financial affairs. This means that any spare cash you have (in your case, cash diverted from Wealth-creating Assets) is used in two stages. First, pay off the home loan; all spare cash should be used for this and nothing should go into investment until the mortgage is gone. Second, when the mortgage is gone, you start to invest.

The order of these things is important. You should pay off the mortgage before you start to invest for two reasons:

- It reduces total indebtedness. As someone on the road to riches you will have other borrowings, and reducing your overall indebtedness will reduce risk.
- You get better returns from repaying debt than you do from Security Assets (which will seldom give you better than 5 per cent after tax and any fees). You are likely to be paying perhaps 8 per cent on the mortgage, which in most countries has to be paid with after-tax income (home loans usually offer little or no tax deductibility of interest payments).

Thus it makes sense to pay off the home loan before you start to invest in Security Assets. This rule does not apply when investing in Wealth-creating Assets, because their rate of return should be 15 per cent or more; much better than the 8 per cent you are likely to be paying on the home loan.

When you have paid off the mortgage on your house you can start building up your other Security Assets.

Chapter 65 | Building a diversified portfolio

The safest investment you can make is a diversified portfolio, a spread of investments across all three asset classes. The idea of a diversified portfolio has been described as the nearest thing an investor ever gets to a free lunch; that's how well it is regarded by investment professionals, who value its safety and steady return. A diversified portfolio contains a mix of investments in the following areas:

- shares;
- property;
- bonds;
- cash; and
- hedge funds.

The last group, hedge funds, refers to a type of mutual fund where the managers put money into sophisticated derivative markets which enable profits to be made when markets are rising or falling. Some of these hedge funds get very good returns, reasonably safely, because of the techniques they use. Some even come with bank guarantees so that after a set time period you are certain to get at least your money back. In this way hedge funds fit very well into a diversified portfolio.

You can either build a diversified portfolio yourself by buying a few shares, some bonds, some property trusts and so on, or you can buy a ready-made diversified portfolio from a fund manager. The best examples of ready-made diversified funds are, of course, superannuation funds; they are nearly always well diversified because the money tends to be invested for the long term and it does need to be safe. The problem with managed funds is, of course, that the fees which are charged eat into your returns. On the other hand, you must take into consideration the convenience and time-saving that managed funds provide—a big advantage when you are trying to focus on your wealth-creating activity.

Building your own diversified portfolio as a Security Asset will take some time, but it may well be something that you enjoy doing. It could also provide a good learning experience. If you do build this portfolio yourself, you have to make sure that you get a very good spread of investments. At the beginning this can be quite difficult, because you only have a small amount to invest and it will not be easy to spread it widely. One of the things you might do is buy into one of the passive index tracker funds. These match the particular index on which they are based (for example, The World Index) and so give a very wide spread of companies for a low amount of investment.

You will also have to be careful as you build your diversified portfolio that it has the correct weighting of assets. The more shares and property securities that you include, the riskier and more volatile your portfolio will be. Therefore, do not over-invest in shares and property; these assets need to be safe, not give performance. No more than 60 per cent of your diversified portfolio should be in shares and property; the balance should be in cash, bonds and hedge funds. Remember also to look for geographical diversification; your Wealth-creating Assets will probably not be spread right around the globe, but you should be looking to invest in Security Assets in Europe or the United States, at least, as well as at home.

Look also to build a portfolio that is a foil to your Wealth-creating Assets. For example, if you are trying to build a chain of computer shops, keep away from investing in high-tech shares; if you are a farmer, do not invest in rural services companies; if you have a growing property investment portfolio, keep clear of property trusts. It is often tempting to invest in the things that you know but in doing so you are putting even more money into the same industry. This is the opposite of what you really need to be doing. You don't want your Security Assets going down at the same time that your Wealth-creating Asset goes wrong.

Chapter 66 | Property investment as a Security Asset

Property can be used as both a Wealth-creating Asset and a Security Asset. How you go about it—what you buy, how much you borrow and how you manage it—depends on your purpose.

	Property for wealth creation	**Property for security**
What to buy:	Price is important (look for a bargain)	Quality is important (good location and tenants)
How much to borrow:	As much as possible	No (or very low) gearing
How to manage:	DIY—very active management	Look for low management (or hire a manager)

The modus operandi of an investor looking for security is quite different from the one who is trying to create wealth. The property for wealth creation needs to be one where rent can be increased and value enhanced, something that can be used to make serious profits which are increased through high leverage. The property as a Security Asset is simply being used as a store for wealth. Good quality property that has little or no borrowings makes a very good Security Asset:

- It is relatively low risk; property markets only seldom crash and good quality property especially shows low volatility.
- Property gives good steady monthly income along with some capital growth.
- The income from good quality property is inflation-proof: over long periods of time the rent is likely to follow at least the rate of inflation (if not a bit more).

Low-geared, good quality property is such a good Security Asset that we often use it as a benchmark against which clients can compare other Security Assets, and even as a test to see if a client has enough for financial freedom.

Our thinking works like this:

We have as clients a couple with a net worth of a little over $1.4 million. This is made up of:

House	$400 000
Business	$900 000
Investments	$100 000

They are in their mid-forties and are still driving their business to greater profitability and value, both working 60 hours a week to do so. They are sick of the long hours, fed up with the business, tired of their lifestyle—they just want to stop!

The business makes a profit of around $200 000 a year before tax. This couple does not have an extravagant or lavish lifestyle, partly because they are too busy but mostly because their tastes and values are simple and home-based. Most of the profits are reinvested in the business. They do not believe they have enough money to be free.

We disagree. We suggest selling the business and using the $900 000 to buy industrial property that will be leased to strong tenants on long-term leases (at least six years). Industrial property is usually bought on a yield of 10 per cent so this should give them around $90 000 p.a. (before tax) in rental return. Industrial property is usually low management and low maintenance, so the couple will have virtually all of the $90 000 on which to live. Over long periods of time the rent should rise at around the rate of inflation, so that even if they do nothing else they should have the spending power today of $90 000 p.a. (before tax) for the rest of their lives.

The point about illustrating the way in which good quality property with no leverage works as a Security Asset is that it is usually very easy for people to imagine themselves with such property. It works because the income from the rents is usually steady, and there is often a feeling of greater control than there is with Security Assets under the care of fund managers. It is also very easy to work out what returns and income there will be—people know how much property their money will buy, and what the rent will be. Property as a Security Asset does at least give a feeling of certainty.

There are risks of course. Property markets do have their ups and downs, tenants do leave and can be hard to replace at times. You will have some management to do (although you could contract this out) and tenants are not always easy to deal with. These risks are alleviated by buying very good quality property (good buildings in good locations, with strong tenants bound by long-term leases) that will require little maintenance, have little need for up-grading, and a very low vacancy rate.

Even if you do not ever plan to put all of your money into property and live off the rent, it does provide a useful benchmark against which you can measure the performance of other Security Assets.

Last word

We were going to finish this book by wishing you good luck. But luck has nothing to do with it. This is in your hands.

If 'luck' does exist it must surely be about the degree to which you are prepared when opportunity strikes. And strike it will! Opportunities arise all the time—daily, weekly, monthly, annually. You probably get the 'opportunity of a lifetime' several times a year. Will you be ready? How well prepared are you to take advantage of the opportunities that will come your way? Many people are overly focused on how difficult times are. But times are always good for those who are prepared and ready to take advantage.

Prepare yourself for sunny days, for good times. You know what you have to do to prepare yourself for rainy days. The real tragedy is to fail to plan for the wonderful things in your life, to not be in a position where you can accept the great opportunities that will most certainly arise.

This is up to you. You can choose to be financially free or choose to be ordinary. The intelligent thing to do is to spend some time to get ready—and then to get out and apply yourself to make the most of the opportunities that await you. You don't have to be an expert or a world-beater to do any of this; you only have to be a bit more prepared than the average person. And you have to be ready and willing to act.

So get yourself ready, get yourself prepared—and go out and make your own luck!